# NiVo 1 • 2012
# Journal for Architecture and Cement Composite

# CONTACT

FibreCem Holding AG
Eternitstrasse 3
CH-8867 Niederurnen

Contact: Anders Holte
T +41 (0)55 617 11 11
nivo@fibre-cem.ch
www.fibre-cem.ch

**SWISSPEARL**®

SWISSPEARL Export
Eternitstrasse 3
CH-8867 Niederurnen

Contact: Liliane Blin
T +41 (0)55 617 11 11
nivo@swisspearl.com
www.swisspearl.com

Photo on previous page:
View from Fridlispitz overlooking Niederurnen

# Here

it is at last! You are now looking at the first edition of the completely new projects journal of the FibreCem Group: **NiVo**. At first sight, perhaps, an unusual name. But in actual fact it has been chosen deliberately. In the first place it should make it clear that this is the works journal of the group as a whole—FibreCem-Holding AG and its subsidiaries Eternit (Schweiz) AG with Swisspearl in **Ni**ederurnen, Switzerland, the ESAL Works in Slovenia, FibreCem Deutschland GmbH, and the Eternit Works Ludwig Hatschek in **Vo**ecklabruck, Austria. Furthermore, the association with the word 'niveau' is no coincidence, since maintaining a high level is—in all modesty—a significant aspect of our corporate philosophy.

Over a century has passed since cement composite was invented by Ludwig Hatschek. In the meanwhile a lot has changed. What remains is the insistence on high quality, which we revise for ourselves every day. Our aim is to work in close partnership with architects, designers and manufacturers on developing trendsetting products and ideas which are convincing both functionally and aesthetically. An architecture journal for the projects has been issued regularly since the 1930s and used both internally and externally as a forum for exchanging ideas and opinions. With NiVo we are continuing that tradition.

However the purpose is not to compete with other architecture journals on the market. This journal rather tries to draw attention to the interactions between architecture, cement composite—from our group of companies—aesthetics, and construction technology. NiVo is still a projects journal: in each edition of NiVo an external, international team of writers and editors will showcase cement composite projects of architectural interest from all over the world. There will also be discussions about the latest developments and approaches to solutions in architecture, placing the projects in the broadest of contexts.

We hope that NiVo will become a platform for an intensive mutual exchange of ideas that will benefit all parties. For that reason, your opinions, your suggestions, and of course your critique will be very important for us.

We look forward to hearing from you.
Yours,
*Anders Holte*

# CONTENT

## 6 MOMENT

The column that features current projects, products and news about cement composite.

'Cement composite' as a stamp: the new reception building on the UNO site in Vienna, by yes architecture, will be the motif of a postage stamp in 2012. The 'Upstanding': the fair stand at the Swissbau 2012 for Eternit AG, designed by Cadosch & Zimmermann Architekten.

## 10 R.S.V.P.

The column with pertinent answers to pertinent questions

The question: 'Why is architecture good advertising?' answered by Nadine Borter, Advertiser of the Year 2011.

## 12 FIRST TIME

A commentary by Dietmar Steiner, Director of the Architecture Centre Vienna, on the beginning of building and the end of publicity.

## 13 DOSSIER: ON YOUR OWN INITIATIVE

'On Your Own Initiative' seeks visionaries, fighters and idealists, faith in the 'common cause', architecture and its image outside the norm.

### 14 Uncommonly Common

Tibor Joanelly in conversation with Miroslav Šik

Opposing the mainstream: Tibor Joanelly spoke with the architect, Miroslav Šik about motives of 'analog architecture' and the common elements in Swiss architecture.

### 20 Constructions

Photo essay by Taiyo Onorato & Nico Krebs

Contrary view: the Swiss artists Taiyo Onorato & Nico Krebs change "analog thoughts and events into images with analog tricks". With their latest series, 'Constructions', they create yet another wonderful sequence of images.

### 28 Verbal Exchange of Blows

Reportage on the 'Fight Club'
Text: Kornel Ringli
Photography: Reiner Riedler

Against complacency: a group of young Viennese architects meets monthly for mutual project criticism.

### 30 Wild at Heart

Studio visit at Vladimir Doray and Vincent Saulier
Text: Manuela Hötzl, Photography: Xavier Mora

Vladimir Dorays' and Vincent Sauliers' 'Wild Club'—vision of a collective statement as utopia.

### 32 Wild Club Session 11/11

Ideas for 'Site' Pont Marie—75004 Paris 2011.

## 37 SITE Morphosis in Shanghai

The campus of the Giant Interactive Group Corporate Headquarters is an artificial landscape with green roofs, lake and park-like recreation areas. A photographic essay of the scene was taken by Iwan Baan.

## 44 REPORT Built for Femininity

Text: Sibylle Hamann
Photography: Katarina Šoškić

How women choose to live: a report about community and communal living from Vienna.

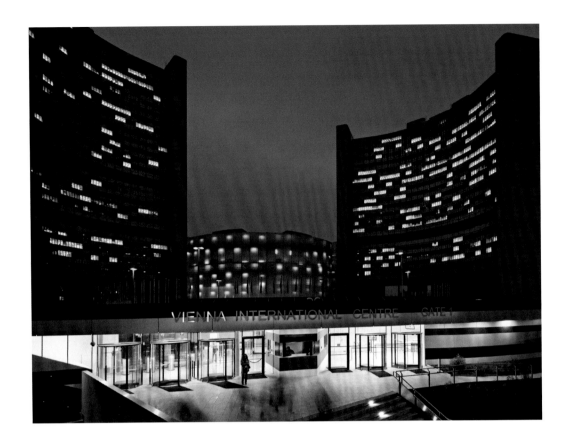

The new UNO City entrance building has a representative character: defining the security, control and scanning zones for employees and visitors. It connects the exterior level of the metro with the higher level of the central Verteiler-Platz.

# Cement Composite as a Stamp

The focal point of Danube City is the Vienna International Centre with its striking office towers. Since 1982 in particular, when the underground station was built, and since 1992, with the master plan by Adolf Krischanitz, building has been constantly ongoing around the 'UNO City'. At present the whole group of buildings is undergoing renewal. Apart from renovation work on the existing structures, at the end of 2011, the new entrance building by yes architecture was opened. The representative building with its facade of fibre cement composite has been chosen to be the motif for a new postage stamp in 2012.

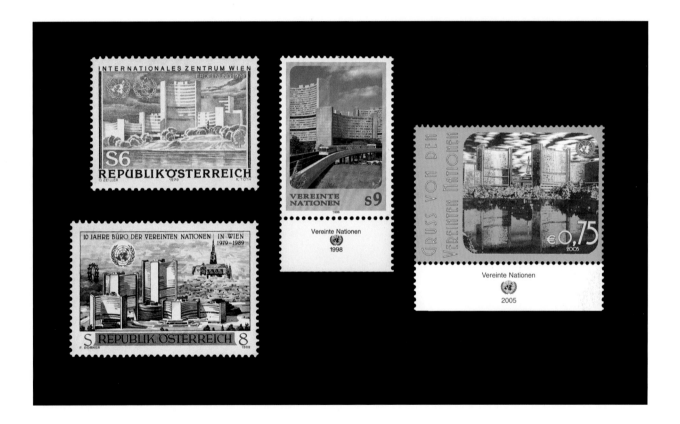

**For** decades Danube City has been one of the biggest urban development areas in Vienna. The centrepiece and symbol of this area located in the south-west of the city between the 'old' and the 'new' Danube is the Vienna International Centre. On a 17-hectare site, six striking office towers were erected with approximately 230,000 square metres of floor space. In 1980, after New York (UNHQ) and Geneva (UNOG), the third official campus of the United Nations (UNOV) began its work. The designer of this highly symbolic building is the little known architect, Johann Staber. In the first round of the architecture competi-

Bespoke postage stamp, Austrian Post
Issued: 1979 and 1989

United Nations Postage Stamps
Issued: 1998 and 2005

tion, in fact, his project was only awarded fourth place. The winning design was by the Argentinian architect, César Pelli, followed by the office of the British BDP Architects and a German firm. Only after it had been revised did the jury, chaired by Roland Rainer, declare the Austrian's project to be the winner. The controversial decision, according to voices in the press at the time, was said to be politically motivated rather than on the basis of architectural quality. To this day, opinions about the building are divided, but there can be no doubt that the building complex has a strong formal presence. Even today—although it has long been surrounded not by green fields but by a densely grown urban area—the six office towers arranged in pairs with a Y-shaped floor plan remain a prominent landmark, visible from a great distance: identity-forming, characteristic and still functional to this day. It is all the more surprising that the architect, Johann Staber, who died in 2005, did not follow it with any well-known projects and left no other relevant architectural work as a legacy, apart from the conference centre 'Austria Centre Vienna (ACV)', an extension of the UNO City.

## yes architecture Makes an Entrance

Even though its formal extroversion is timeless, the conditions in the urban context have changed radically since the UNO City was erected. Now that it has its own underground railway station, not only has the frequency and number of UNO City visitors risen, but indeed the entire accessibility and the entrance situation have had to be reorganised. After all, it was also necessary to adjust to the new regulations regarding the requirements of security technology. All that led to a competition for a new entrance building for the United Nations, which the architects, Marion Wicher and Ruth Berkhold from yes architecture, were able to win. The expansion of the new entrance was structured for the daily flow of visitors, up to 8,000 people on several levels that defined the security, control and scanning

zones for staff and visitors. Designing logistical processes with spatial efficiency and layering the various levels of security form the core function of the building: the visitors' centre ($700\,\text{m}^2$) and the 'scanning zone' ($550\,\text{m}^2$) have thus been organised more straightforwardly and, at the same time, more clearly separated from each other. In addition, the entrance building should also show a representative appearance and connect the outside level of the underground railway with the higher central distribution area of the site.

## New Curved Forms

The technical challenge for the architects was the site itself. The building was, in fact, erected over an existing underground parking garage from the 1970s, the structure of which was not designed for this purpose. A decision was made, consequently, in favour of a steel frame structure fitted with light or solid walls as required. In some places the material had to be optimised for its function of providing protection from bullets and bombs. Formally, the office towers and their Y-form are downgraded; the entrance building reaches out towards visitors with rounded forms. In addition the facade takes up the horizontal structure of the exiting material and provides variety with bands of cement composite in various colours.

## The Stamp

Even after its opening in 1979, the UNO City was the motif of a postage stamp, as it was again in the jubilee year of 1989, and now, with the finalisation of the new entrance building, the powerful brand 'UNO' and its architecture create the basis for an edition in this small format publication.

Text: Manuela Hötzl (MaHo)

# Cement Composite as a Brand

The biannual event, Swissbau, took place from 17 to 21 January 2012 in Basel where the most prestigious of the Swiss building and real estate industries displayed both their new and their tried-and-tested wares. Eternit (Switzerland) AG held a presentation with Swisspor AG on a combined stand.

**The** architects, Cadosch & Zimmermann, acting for both subsidiaries of FibreCem Holding AG, designed an astonishingly homogeneous landscape using the high-performance insulation material EPS and wall tiles of cement composite. The organic world of forms at the 400-square-metre pavilion was a real eye-catcher. Visitors could expect insights into the optical quality of the anthracite-coloured insulation material and the typical colour range of cement composite. The sweeping curves of the bars, parapets and roof terminations were made of the anthracite-coloured insulation. Yes, you have read that correctly. Under the name 'swissporLAMBDA' the enterprise displayed an innovative system product

for insulating metal boxes, developed in cooperation with the market. In addition to providing more effective insulation, like all materials from expanded polystyrene, it can be wholly recycled. The eco-balance-sheet of its entire life cycle is one of the best, especially when you take its powerful insulation performance into account.

The decision to use it for the Swissbau was, however, based more on the fact that EPS can be shaped freely as desired in each case. In other words, it was less a matter of showing the actual use of the material than of fascinating architects with the way the insulation material can be used for unexpected purposes. The intention was to give the stand a unified form while using the two basic materials, EPS and cement composite. Underlying this were the

four oval wooden structures, which were clad with wall tiles. Due to its fully matured application techniques the roofing tiles have a wide range of applications: 15 formats in 28 colours can be mounted all around the building—even on curved surfaces, as the Swissbau stand showed. With their ruby, topaz and amber tints, the small rectangular tiles created an iridescent appearance, which was emphasised even more by the dark strips of EPS. Due to back-lit textile coverings the latter looked like feathery tiles. It is a shame that the spaceship-like stand glided away again a few days after its brief stopover in Basel.

Text: Kornel Ringli (KoRi)

11 We only have to open a magazine and look at the adverts to realise: architecture is also suitable for advertising, whether as background to an image or to represent a firm. And yet the product or firm being advertised quite often has nothing at all to do with architecture. This brings us to a thesis: when architecture and marketing are combined meaningfully with each other, a building can represent the firm's identity to the outside world. What conclusions can be drawn about the company from the design, materials and symbolic programme of a building?

# Why is Architecture Good Advertising?

Nadine Borter, the Swiss advertiser of the year 2011, general manager and proprietor of the Contexta AG advertising agency, responds:

A good business enterprise must use every kind of communication medium to advertise itself. This includes the way it looks, which is partly determined by its architecture. Not only good architecture, even bad architecture can be good advertising. While a firm like Vitra underlines its design competence with buildings by Zaha Hadid or Herzog & de Meuron, the discount retailer Aldi, with its barracks-style architecture, makes it clear to every visitor, leaving no room for misunderstanding, that every dollar counts. In both cases architecture is used cleverly for its particular purpose.

Projects like, for example, the Novartis Campus are harder to place in the scheme of things—an architectural El Dorado that is largely concealed from the public. And yet here too, architecture is good advertising. Not so much for outsiders as for insiders: the world's best architecture is used to advertise for the world's best staff. Agencies have also discovered the value of good architecture. A good example is Jay Chiat, who commissioned Frank O. Gehry to build the futuristic Chiat/Day Building in 1985. No-one who comes through its doors will doubt that the most creative minds in the country work there.

The importance of architecture for the image and success of a firm, however, should not be overestimated. For example, Apple was able to turn itself into a world brand with an architecturally-speaking fairly modest headquarters. Not until shortly before his death, and at the high point of his success, did Steve Jobs commission the architect, Norman Foster to plan a new, spectacular corporate building. This shows us: architecture is used not so much to make successful advertising, as to proudly celebrate success.

In the next edition of NiVo, Nadine Borter asks the Swiss architecture and design theoretician, Arthur Rüegg: How does a piece of furniture become a design classic?

First work by Aldo Rossi, summer cottage, 1960
Marina di Massa, Localitá Ronchi, via Fichi

**The** original idea at this point was a presentation of the 'first work' of a universally known and famous architect. Those approached all turned us down. Considering their present careers, it seems as if they did not want to be reminded of their humble beginnings.

For every architect at some point the 'first time', the first commission, will come. This first job is of decisive importance for the beginning of a professional career. For the first commission assumes an enormous level of trust on the part of the client. After all, a building is to be erected with a planner who has never done it before on his or her own responsibility. It is indeed the first time. Many architects remain grateful to their first client for the rest of their lives, because they developed that sense of trust. Quite right, too. Would you trust a tradesman or a doctor who was putting her learnt theoretical knowledge into practice for the first time?

But in that case, isn't it deep ingratitude when one denies that first piece of work at the high point of one's career? After all, the first commission can determine the course of later fields of work, or it can be called a failure due to inexperience. Is it permissible to remain silent about the parts of a creative career that one sees as dark? Is it even possible in the age of digitally scrutinised life?

The real problem behind this ludicrous act of resistance concerns the entire matter of architectural publicity, and it has been growing now for several years. One upon a time, architectural media selected and publicised buildings and projects by criteria relating to their contents, their qualities or their themes. The architects felt honoured, made plans and descriptions available, and editors commissioned photographers. But even in the 1990s star architects—and those who wanted to be stars—tried to have total control over the publication of their works. Waiting

periods were introduced for the press, because agreements had been signed with individual media for exclusive publication. The projects were to be photographed only by specified photographers and authors were sought out by the architects and given releases.

We need to take note of this development. There is no longer any such thing as autonomous reporting on architecture, buildings and projects. There are now only well-meaning repetitions of the authorised self-declarations of architects. Media have become marketing platforms for architects, and exhibition halls are now the same. Whether this desire for total control can be sustained in the age of Web 2.0 may, however, be doubted. The 'Ministries of Home Protection' in firms of architects have not yet found out that they have been surpassed by media technology…

Text: Dietmar Steiner

# ON YOUR OWN INITIATIVE

# ON YOUR OWN INITIATIVE

'On Your Own Initiative' is not about the lonely architect cowboy riding into the desert on the wave of whatever is new and trendy—and still claiming to save the world. This is not about the most beautiful, biggest and best—and not about a star cult. 'On Your Own Initiative' is rather a matter of searching for the idea in the 'common matter' of architecture. For even though architecture has come to a point where architects are increasingly driven more by personal commitment than economic interest—a higher goal, extending beyond the next project, is rarely pursued. The following pages provide evidence that alternative models to this image of the profession are available, so that people can experiment 'on their own initiative' to react to the mainstream by opposing it in some way. One architect is the most eloquent champion of the Analog Architecture movement, Miroslav Šik. The architecture theorist, Tibor Joanelly spoke with Šik about formative predecessors in Modernism, the desire for holistic architecture and what really drives the debate about architecture in Switzerland today.

    With actions somewhat closer to actual practice comes the Viennese 'Fight Club', which has been formed by a few young architectural teams and which meets every month to critique each other's projects.

    No less structurally, but far more informally, the 'Wild Club' by-passes standardised competition processes and hierarchies. The French architects, Vladimir Doray and Vincent Saulier, explain why and describe their 'wild' vision of the architect's life.

    The Swiss artists, Taiyo Onorato & Nico Krebs, try in all their works "to transform thoughts and events into images with analog tricks". With their latest series, *Constructions*, they have once again created a wonderful sequence of images.

    The dossier 'On Your Own Initiative' adds something more to the accustomed image, devoting itself to the 'Heroes of Everyday Life', the fighters and idealists. In this way, NiVo—Journal for Architecture and Cement Composite—determines the path its contents will follow: showing architecture through the heterogeneity of its protagonists and, in doing so, listening more closely to the finer nuances, over and beyond the mainstream.

Manuela Hötzl, Kornel Ringli
Editors of NiVo

Miroslav Šik takes a consistently critical position
about the promises of Modernism.

# Uncommonly Common

Miroslav Šik is regarded as one of the founders and the most vocal defendant of 'Analog architecture'. In the interview below he explains what circumstances and interests were behind this movement, which started at the Swiss Federal Institute of Technology Zurich (ETH Zurich) and was central to the Swiss realm of architecture in the 1980s; distinguishing it from the design mainstream. Šik sets out the declarations that are still, in their core, virulent and significant—and thus represents a position that continues to be critical about the promises of Modernism.

Tibor Joanelly interviewed Miroslav Šik

**Tibor Joanelly (TJ):** In an interview you made with Axel Simon and Hendrik Tieben you spoke, in connection with the beginnings of 'Analog Architecture', about a certain deliberate distance from what was then mainstream architecture at the ETH Zurich. What distancing strategies did you use at that time?

**Miroslav Šik (MS):** The situation around 1983/84, which gave rise to 'Analog Architecture', was very heterogeneous and diffused. On the one hand, there was the world of Aldo Rossi. The resulting architecture, namely imitations of Maestro Rossi's style, didn't satisfy us, in spite of the analytical drills in the ETH atelier of Campe and Rossi, when dealing with urban design and its history. It contradicted the idea that originally fascinated us: in that architecture is to be filtered out from its contextual surroundings. At that time, I would say, Rossi's approach was already being studied critically by his acolytes and students—which should probably be brought back to Rossi's own door. The idea that one should question the city where one lives and works—its history and its design qualities—was to remain important for 'Analog Architecture'. On the other hand, there was at that time still some late Modernism, represented perhaps by the generation of Dolf Schnebli, and it was not especially powerful and had little fascination for us. At the same time there were also the tendencies from Ticino: their elegance and the relationship to Modernism did interest us. I mean, at the beginning of 'Analog Architecture' the critical lesson already applied. Somehow fascinated by the Ticino tendencies, and due—this should not be forgotten—to Rossi's references to the enchanting Modernism of the Mediterra-

nean, we discovered the Modernism of the pre-war and post-war periods with their regional and historical variety in quite a different way.

**TJ:** At that time, was the 'Casa del Fascio', Italian 'razionalismo', the determining factor with which one could establish one's distance from Schnebli's way of understanding Modernism?

**MS:** With his moderate, luke-warm Corbusier Modernism, Schnebli was left behind. This was unsatisfactory for us, not only as Russians, but also as slow discoverers of Modernism. The field was open. There was no articulated position in German-Swiss architecture. This gap was filled by the positions of the Ticino tendencies and of us as the second generation of Russians. When we set out with our first designs, a kind of passing Postmodernism à la IBA Berlin 1984 was the order of the day. Hardly had we learned Rossi's style than it was already a bit passé for us, and we looked for another kind of expression. My fellow colleagues went even further then, and their search led to the positions of Neo-Modernism.

**TJ:** At that time, you and your colleagues shared a drawing style based on Rossi's 'città analoga'—was this a means to distinguish oneself?

**MS:** It needs to be emphasised that, at the time we are talking about, Rossi did not use a realistic art of representation. On the contrary, he used a kind of collage. That was no longer the black-and-white, the devilish, that had caught our attention before. Hardly had we become aware of him then he changed to a pleasant, yellow-blue pastel colouring, quoting himself. For us it was the starting point for a critical appropriation. Neither should we forget that the films of Jim Jarmusch and Wim Wenders were running

Where Mediterranean Modernism can be found in a unique way:
The Cemetery of San Cataldo by Aldo Rossi.

Konrad Hürlimann, semester job for a car dealer in
Zürich Oerlikon, 1987

Miroslav Sik, competition project for the tele-
communications building in Zürich-Binz, 1986.

in cinemas at that time, with a black-and-white submersion into the trivial or peripheral. I think some of us allowed ourselves to be fascinated by Neo-Modernism and some of us would simply take from Rossi what he had shown us in Chioggia and in Milan's industrial landscape: fascination with rural ancillary buildings and the industrial buildings in the fog of early modernisation. In our drawings, we experimented. The first representation we tried out was classical Russian: a white facade, square windows and a background sprayed with a toothbrush. Black and white, incredibly precise, extremely clean, nobody else was drawing like that. And then colour came in slowly; that was probably initiated by Rossi himself. With Jaxon chalk that he had brought with him from America, he made the sky blue over the buildings and made the buildings yellow. For the first time, colour became an option. Even for our graduation work we made our plans look like pictures, big, perfectly precise, with clinically accurate lines. About that time alternative students

> **We had an urge for completeness; the 'Dirty' in 'Dirty Realism' as an architecture that had discovered the worn out, the trivial for itself, which is now exhausted.**

drew a bit with soft, 2B pencils on yellowish-brownish paper, using light, trembling lines, a bit shaded, beautiful things, a work in progress—but everything was sketchy. For our graduation we framed the drawings, carried the lines on to the edge, to the bitter end. For our first competition projects, such as the Papierwerd-Areal, we tried out big perspectives with pen and ink or with airbrush.

**TJ:** I could now say something provocative: that nothing remains of 'Analog Architecture' apart from the intensity of the drawing. Is there anything that goes on living over and beyond the drawing?

**MS:** The representative style of the first Analogs has died out. We had an urge for completeness; the 'Dirty' in 'Dirty Realism' as an architecture that had discovered the worn out, the trivial for itself, is now exhausted. But what is left is the fundamental theme of blending the classics with 'Dirty Realism'. The core idea was and is to make a kind of 'Bobo Architecture'; a blend of alternative, bohemian and bourgeois moods, following the attribute 'Bobo', which goes back to the book *Bobos in Paradise* by David Brooks, published in 2000. 'Bobo' stands for bohemian-bourgeois. 'Bobo Architecture' is somewhat conventional and somewhat alternative. You mix a bourgeois palazzo with a loft. The Analogs discovered the basic blend at that time. That is far more important than representation. You can see that again and again in current architecture: a building should be modern, but at the same time fit into its context; it should seem conventional and alternative at once. These days that is an incredibly virulent kind of design. The blend is probably of interest to middle-class, educated élite strata, because they demonstrate the 'bobo' in the way they

live. Before they want any kind of design from us, they are living in a middle-class house in the city with a nice oak parquet, with plaster rosettes on the ceiling and with panelling on the lower part of the wall, made of wood—but they put a few clean, cool and designed objects into the living rooms. With this mixture in their everyday lives, people want modernity, but they also want antiquity, the tried and tested and inherited old world. But for most people that is not blended in the art object, but they have a modern car and an old house and drive away for retro-holidays. I believe that this mixture of moods is the most important theme in modern living: old and new, warm and cool, noblesse and vulgar, regional and exotic …

**TJ:** You talk of an aesthetic of everyday life. For my own part, I always ask myself: how can the everyday be translated into architecture?

**MS:** We need to remind ourselves that we live in a country with a very sophisticated discussion about architecture and—due to the Reform movement and the Werkbund—in a country with a very sophisticated culture of objects. If we start with the everyday, it is doubtless a very polished one. It is represented by everyday objects, but also by everyday institutions, such as housing cooperatives and building committees. In them you can find imprints from the apartment reform movements of the 20th century as well as those of the avant-garde. That is not the case in every country. In other words: if we were really to follow Venturi in the way he meant it in his book *Learning from Las Vegas*, we would also have to take account of the excesses, we would have to include the banal everyday world of commerce—but I am convinced that that world is not the dominant one in Switzerland. It exists, it is ugly, but it does not control culture. Today I can still negate the IKEA and Baumarkt world in the suburbs of Zurich and say: most of the building production is admittedly not beautiful, but it is not absolute

> **Most of the building production is admittedly not beautiful, but it is not absolute ugliness either. Good, solid building still happens, with good materials and with an eye to the long term.**

ugliness either. Good, solid building still happens, with good materials and with an eye to the long term. Since the mainstream is in fact very sophisticated, we can afford to start there, encircle it and also ennoble it a little. But I notice—since I now live with one foot in Prague—that I revert to the old elitist attitude there and don't want to take over anything at all from the everyday, because it is crass, blatant, noisy, exaggerated, intrusive.

**TJ:** What is really common, therefore, is a threat to the uncommonly common?

**MS:** Yes. Again: the commercial, the cheap, the retro-restaurants, the clothing one wears twice or thrice a year and then throws away, you can find all that here, too. But

the chaotic and instantaneous are not the rule. Additive urban design in Switzerland is admittedly also additive, but it is still put together quite nicely with green patches or very sound streets. As time passes all the fragments fit together to make an ensemble, and that now happens more or less in modern quarters. I have never seen it quite like that on the periphery of Paris, nor in Moscow or Prague; there the modern simply stands there, with its fragments and specimens, with their absolute, brutal, capitalist power.

**TJ:** Perhaps the danger in Switzerland is rather the opposite: that, to put it this way, the knowledgeable exalts the little things and robs them of their beauty by doing so?

**MS:** Of course. But I think the big danger is that things will remain common. After all, we have always said that it is about the magic of things. One has to make them

### But I think the big danger is that things will remain common.

a little bit nobler. People need to take note of what is small and beautiful, consciously and with pride, they must deliberately take care of it—otherwise things wither. Otherwise they lose their milieu, their heart's blood and their homeliness, one stops even noticing them—and then Switzerland will become boring, the gray and standardised will take over and 'excesses' will no longer be possible. The danger is that the common will stay common. Or, of course, the reverse: when the mainstream satisfies claims that are too high, there is a possibility that the little things will no longer have a place; they will be pushed aside by luxury. And so in recent times as

the *dernier cri* people have been buying that charming Danish furniture of the post-war modern, where every piece costs a huge amount; a chair costs 2,000 Swiss francs or more.

**TJ:** When you talk about ennobling and caring for things, you sound like a gardener …

**MS:** Swiss architecture owes a great deal to the relationship between people and the landscape, their territory. That is why a large number of villages become part of the agglomeration; the buildings are not related to each other—but the inhabitants care for the spaces in between in a very rustic or romantic-gentle way. Here there is an ability to keep to the cultivated medium. In hardly any other country are so many trees planted at the same time as a building goes up. Almost everyone plants himself a tree and covers the building a little bit with bushes and climbers. The decoration and the citation are not so obtrusively explicit and low maintenance is not everyone's thing either. That means that people have to understand something about their landscape and its natural qualities—I suppose it comes from their ancestors. The negatively intended remark that every Swiss is a peasant is something rather positive for me. They probably understand the seasons, what grows well, nature in its variety. The average citizen in the European metropolises no longer knows anything about his landscape, at best he sees it as a background to holidays or as something to be exploited …

**TJ:** Now we have praised the average Swiss to excess. Where could one apply the barb?

**MS:** I have the impression that capitalism in urban design and architecture is still deregulated—in spite of the building laws. There is still an inability to see building primarily as a matter of dealing with long-term and permanent

A black-and-white dive into the trivial:
*Stranger than Paradise* by Jim Jarmusch.

Designer pieces as *dernier cri* obscure the little things.

needs. Buildings are put up so that someone makes money and leases something out. This attitude to urban design and architecture is still very dangerous. And yet today, as much as ever, interesting questions are posed: how do we react to the problems of mobility, with new citizens coming to us from other countries? Not calmly, in a regulated way, but suddenly there are large-scale settlements and their density is too great. I have the impression that the idea of freedom in Switzerland also creates problems and that planning and design are too weak as an instrument to oppose it. Too often things are still permitted that are purely egoistic and relate to nothing.

> **I have the impression that the idea of freedom in Switzerland also creates problems and that planning and design are too weak as an instrument to oppose it. Too often things are still permitted that are purely egoistic and relate to nothing.**

The second very big danger for Switzerland is that it orients itself towards luxury, so that demands constantly increase. They are already so high in relation to urban design quality and to architectural and technical accessories that ordinary people have little opportunity to express themselves in architecture. But that is something they need to do—when you see where they go for their holidays. We really must build according to the context and natural evolution, we must stop the processes that are destroying the countryside. Even today we have not yet gained control of flight from the country and flight from the city. I have always spoken of the 'Little Big City'—but the tendency is simply to Big City and agglomeration. The village and the small town as qualities and as counterparts to the big cities will disappear. The process of large-scale urbanisation simply continues—people are not aware that the true quality is 'Little Big City'. They want to have their ennoblement, at least to perfect their level in life, they demand every kind of economic growth and modernisation, which results in even more urbanisation taking place. Urban design as an ensemble no longer occurs and the city edges go on fraying. In spite of the quality of the buildings, in spite of the careful construction of roads and of green patches, we are losing what really belongs to a Swiss city: town and country together. And the danger of this process can also be seen there: that one simply goes on and on in little steps and with the best intentions … but, oh well, that is simply Swiss!

Tended ordinariness in
the agglomeration.

Miroslav Šik (*1953) is an architect and theorist in Zurich. He graduated under Aldo Rossi and Mario Campi at the ETH Zurich and since 1999 he has himself been a professor there. Since the beginning of the 1990s Miroslav Šik has been seen as the founder of 'Analog Architecture', one of the "moving, renewing and questioning spirits in the Swiss and the German-language debate about architecture."
Publications: *Analoge Architektur*, Edition Boga, 1988; *Altneu*, Miroslav Šik, Quart Verlag, 2000; *Altneue Gedanken. Texte und Gespräche 1987–2001*, Quart Verlag, 2002.

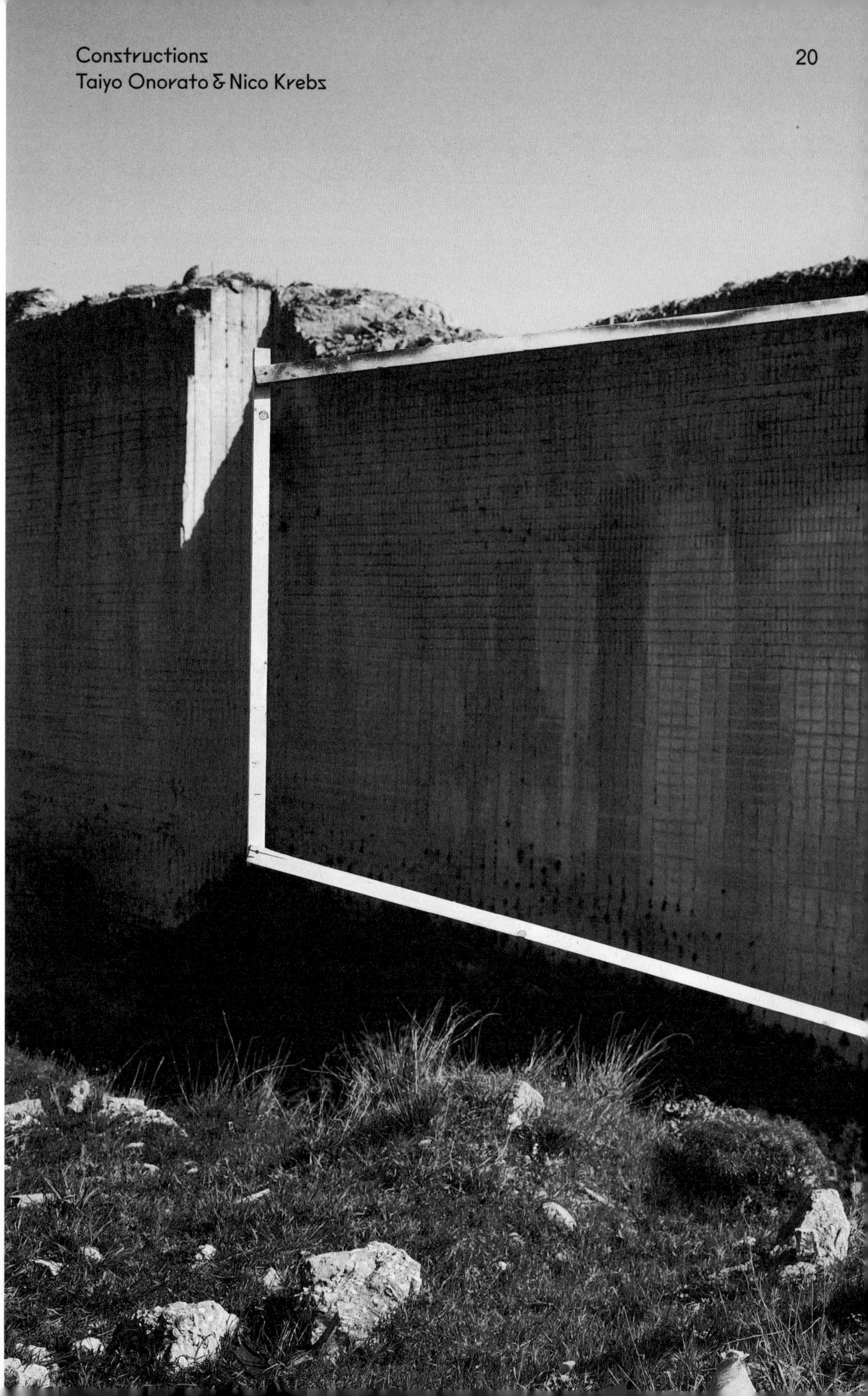

# Verbal Exchange of Blows

A group of young Viennese architects meets every week to critique each other's projects. In a profession better known for its vanities than its critical skills, the Fight Club seems quite exotic.

Text: Kornel Ringli
Photography: Reiner Riedler

**Archi**tects are often vain. They practice their art aesthetically and like to present their well-designed projects in well-designed books and, without consideration for the size of their work catalogue, they want it published sooner rather than later. They have their completed works photographed by professionals—definitely before the owner's tasteless chattels have obscured the signs of architectural genius. And, finally, the resulting images are submitted to the specialist journals, no matter how insignificant the object might be. Anyone who pursues his career so insistently and so unrelentingly sees even the most average addition to their parent's home as a creative masterpiece.

Fight Club with Erwin Stättner (Franz Architekten), Markus Bösch and Bernd Scheffknecht (YF Architekten), Christoph Leitner (Plov Architekten), Michael Wildmann and Irene Prieler (Grundstein)

## Twenty-two eyes see more than four

Self-love is also expressed in architects through their avoidance of criticism. They react to defeats in competitions by feeling offended: it was all the jury's fault; they misunderstood the architectural miracle. During competitions, more than ever, visitors are not gladly welcomed to the office. The architect is not willing to have someone see the cards in his hand. That this does not have to be the case is shown by the Fight Club. This loose collection of a few young Viennese architectural firms does not shy away from mutual criticism. On the last Friday of every month they meet for an exchange of verbal blows: "I'd never sit down there!" says one of the participants about a bench in a school corridor which, in his opinion, is much too dark. "Why did you abandon the rounded form? It's neither fish nor fowl. The interior will never work like that—all those empty spaces!" The person under attack puts up his defenses: "I really don't understand what you're talking about. We checked it in the film—and anyway, this construction is much simpler." Another participant talks about the facade: "Airy and light is fine for me, but inside … can't those posts simply be left out?" And then, as the discussion is in danger of cooling off, one of the project's authors asks provocatively: "All right? Can we tender it like that?" Not yet quite: "Ten fire zones … ten of them!" a debater questions whether the project complies with the building laws.

In many cases the participants are familiar with projects from earlier Fight Clubs so that only a short introduction is needed before getting down to business. But it can happen that the speaker doesn't even get to the actual question in hand. "How does your escape route work?" someone interrupts the project introduction with the result that his colleagues also start grappling with the question. This is perfectly acceptable, since it confronts the debaters with unexpected objections of the kind they encounter in their everyday professional lives. "The Fight Club trains our conversational skills and our ability to explain things," says Erwin Stättner from Franz Architekten. "It makes us fitter verbally for dealing with unaccustomed situations in discussions with clients." This helps the younger firms especially to find the appropriate design and negotiating strategy—and it has already proven valuable, in particular in competitions. They often speak of a two-stage process, which was ultimately won with the help of constructive criticism in the Fight Club. In this way the participating firms benefit from the experiences of each other. "Our school building has smaller windows and yet lighting is still not a problem," so that doubts can be laid to rest. Suddenly someone asks about safety from break-ins, whereupon an architect who has experience with school buildings replies that this is not a problem in this case, as she can assume from previous experience. Usually the suggestions made by the Fight Club are not simply taken over, one on one, into the project, but the criticism stimulates the other participant to think: were we quite safe with our solution on this corner?

Were we too hasty about our decision to place the wardrobes on the upper floor? Twenty-two eyes see more than four. The Fight Club gives full meaning to the empty slogan from creativity research, "Thinking outside the box".

## 'Letting It All Out'

This was the original idea of the Fight Club. When one of the founding members of Franz Architekten left, his unconventional ideas, wild fantasies and internal discussions were also missed; the two remaining partners, Robert Diem and Erwin Stättner, were too similar and they felt the absence of a critical voice. Three years ago, that was the starting point for drumming fellow students and work colleagues together to hold the first Fight Club. Since then a hard core of five firms—apart from Franz, there are YF Architekten, plov, Sue and Grundstein—come together for an architectural wrestling match. "Just letting it all out, once a month," is how Stättner describes the pleasure he takes in the Fight Club, and by that he means the opportunity to debate about architecture outside everyday office life. Without time pressure or financial pressure, armed with rolls of plans, models, sample materials and the like one goes into a fight that is regulated with just a few debating rules: the highest priority rule is to express an honest opinion. "If we spent our time beating around the bush, no-one would benefit from it," the debaters declare unanimously. Secondly: no finished projects. The Fight Club does not see itself as a spiritualised debating circle but as a work group, there to solve specific practical problems or to get around them cleverly.

## A Constant Breath of Fresh Air

As in the film of the same name, therefore, the Fight Club is also a self-organised combination for tackling problems together, but the group is by no means a secret lodge. Usually about a dozen architects turn up, but industrial designers have also come at times, and the civil engineer Christian Petz is usually present as well. Variety is good and provides new excitement, those present agree. "A breath of fresh air is always welcome." At 7 p.m. it gets going, in a different office each time. It is not necessary to say you are coming, but it is preferred—so that the right amount of refreshments can be provided. The Fight Club also has a social dimension. After two hours of debating someone shouts "Sausage time!" Water is put on to boil, frankfurters are lowered into it, and then they are eaten. When it starts up again—it is past ten o'clock—another project is held up for criticism. Two or three projects are examined each evening before the last round of the match is rung in with 'Rossbacher' herb liqueur. The relaxed atmosphere seems to contribute to a free and easy exchange of ideas. The Fight Club creates the conditions for an unconventional partnership of colleagues. "We could never work as an office team," says Markus Bösch from YF Architekten, "we have completely different work styles."

# Wild at Heart

Vladimir Doray and Vincent Saulier had a vision of an architects' life outside the mainstream and of a 'different' architecture. These two architects wanted to combine with their generation against the father-figure Le Corbusier and find a new path together that would lead to a new architectural language. What remains from their collective statement, as both utopia and fun, is the 'Wild Club'.

Text: Manuela Hötzl

**The** rat-race of a career in architecture, consisting of competitions lost and won, 'Europan', this or that exhibition and ultimately the founding of a firm with the knowledge that "you can survive but not live from it", does not just begin with the—usually late—graduation day. The situation for French architects is no different from that of their other European colleagues. "To gain access to competitions or be invited to take part in them is practically impossible for a young architect in France," says Vincent Saulier, "you have to have a comprehensive portfolio very early to be able to make a proper start." One ticket to get into the architecture scene is to publish in *NAJAP* (Les nouveaux albums des jeunes architectes & des paysagistes)—called 'Album' for short. If you are represented there with your work, you have made the first major step towards public recognition. But it is not easy to be accepted into the 'Album network'. Founded in 2002 by the Ministry for Culture and Communications, a jury selects a group of architects and landscape designers aged under 35, biannually, from more than 200 participants who deserve the "visibility and recognition", as the French Minister of Culture Frédéric Mitterrand describes the criteria.

## Wild or Serious

The architecture scene and its portfolios are constant topics of discussion between Vladimir Doray and Vincent Saulier. At last Vladimir Doray managed to get into the *2007/2008 NAJAP* book, partly with a joint project, which also gave his firm its name: Wild Rabbit Architecture'. Vincent had passed the age ceiling, which also meant that he missed out on the success balance sheet for 2007/2008: in two years, according to François de Mazières (Cité de l'architecture et du patrimoine), the 20 selected firms took part in 229 competitions, were awarded 53 private commissions, participated in 74 exhibitions, managed a list of 165 publications and conferences and also received 16 prizes or honours.

We are sitting in the atrium of Vladimir Doray's courtyard house in the north of Paris, not far from the Parc de la Villette, surrounded by a dense layer of buildings—no traffic noise can filter in here, nor sunbeams on this hot day in October 2011. In the courtyard one is surrounded by an entire daily course of events, concentrated into a few square metres. Kitchen and living room in one corner—in a side annex an office of about 15 square metres, where Vladimir works with his three assistants. The fourth side is enclosed by a wall, with a mini-biotope in front of it, including a small toad—in short, an inwardly focused urban oasis.

> **"It no longer has anything to do with architecture. It has become more like art, actionism, a picture party."**

A copy of the Wild Club exhibition catalogue lies on the table. The show took place in 2010 at the Pavillon de l'Arsenal, with an overview of the past two years. The basic idea of the Wild Club is simple: each month a picture of a site is sent to more than 1,000 members, and they have 24 hours to send it back with their concept. The pictures of places, plots of land or city views are selected by Vladimir Doray, sent out and documented on the website. The contributions range from simply presented ideas, illustrations or even comics to considered designs and suggested projects. Some people take part regularly in the Wild Club, while others turn up only once and disappear from the scene again. Criticism is rarely uttered; once a member wanted of his own initiative to have all of his contributions deleted ("He justified that by saying that he had insulted colleagues with his designs," Doray smilingly explains the incident).

The sessions have been taking place since May 2008. The collection from three years of Wild Club includes only a few designs for buildings. Why that is so? "I wouldn't call the contributions serious. Neither in their presentation nor in their content. It no longer has anything to do with architecture. It has become more like art, actionism, a picture party," Vladimir Doray explains. The original idea was different and had very serious intentions: to achieve more professional skills by practicing design regularly. Doray: "I knew back then that my designs work very well—but I couldn't say that they were clever or good architecture." In addition to practicing design, they both wanted to learn from each other and from the others, in both content and graphic skills. The combined portfolio was intended to be nothing more than a side-effect of the process.

## In the Shadow of Le Corbusier

When Vladimir Doray and Vincent Saulier first met, at the end of their studies in the drawing room for undergraduates at the Ecole Nationale Supérieure d'Architecture de Paris-Belleville, they were asking themselves about the future: "What will we do when we are really doing architecture?" This by no means unusual, though also a rather naive question started a debate between the two about the profession of architecture and the urge to determine their everyday architectural lives for themselves. "At the university we were brought up to be Le Corbusier's 'great-nephews'. That is how we were to draw, to draft and to think. It's no wonder we were looking for something else," says Doray. By working together they came to realise how fruitful teamwork can be. Vladimir was the analyst, Vincent the graphic designer. Vincent Saulier: "But we wanted to extend our horizons, to think and act in larger categories and contexts."

Their first joint competition for a housing block outside Paris was then to bring up even more specific architectural questions. Doray's and Saulier's vision for the competition was a green-biased building landscape with atria, courtyards and roof terraces, dug into the earth. Because people living in high-rise buildings are called 'rabbits' in France, their project was given the name Wild Rabbits.

Even now, as one looks back nostalgically, it becomes clear how seriously they meant it all at the time when, as a next step, they called on other architects, friends and colleagues to take part in the competition together. Their idea was to present contributions on various sites in various countries by various architects as a joint concept. The Europan jury was expected to understand: there is a group of people out there who think alike, present their drafts in the same way and speak of the same things—and do not step up to the mark as competitors.

The intention was on a large scale, and so was the effort of organisation—those project failed. Apart from Vladimir and Vincent none of those invited submitted their plans. The reason was that even the question of what to name the authors or how to create uniform layouts did not help the experiment—what is more, there was not enough time to reach agreement. The commitment and the vision to figure a scene remained all the same. "In spite of all that, I still did not want to give up the basic idea of exchanging ideas," is how Vladimir explains his unflagging optimism—and the founding of the Wild Club.

Unlike Vincent, who delivers his contribution almost every month, Vladimir himself no longer takes part in the Wild Club—but in spite of the many competitions he works on with his team, he has found a new form of practice for himself: he gives long-vanished kinds of architecture a new history, as the fictitious, drawn biography of a building. A project—just for himself alone.

Site: Pont Marie – 75004 Paris
© Xavier Mora

Image: Atelier Portátil
Title: Seed Us

Image: Laurent Poggio

Image: Diane Berg

# Les règles du Wild Club

1 —  Il est permis de parler du Wild Club.

2 —  Il est permis au Wild Club de diffuser les projets présentés.

3 —  Le projet dure 24h, si quelqu'un dit stop ou s'évanouit, le projet continue.

4 —  Les participants projettent quand ils peuvent pendant la session en cours.

5 —  Un site à la fois, pas de programme imposé, pas de PLU à respecter.

6 —  Tous les outils sont permis, toutes formes d'équipes sont bienvenues.

7 —  L'insertion du projet dans l'image du site est le seul document exigé.

8 —  Il n'y a pas d'autre règle, pas de classement, pas de récompense.

## www.wildclub.be

Rules of 'Wild Club'

1 —  It's allowed to talk about the 'Wild Club'.
2 —  It's allowed for the Wild Club to broadcast introduced plans.
3 —  The project lasts 24h, if someone says stop or blacks out, the project goes on.
4 —  Everyone develops their project anytime during the curent session.
5 —  One site, no compulsory program, no urban rules to respect.
6 —  All tools are allowed, all teams welcome.
7 —  The integration of the project in the site's picture is the only required document.
8 —  There are no other rules, no grades, no rewards.

# Built
# Femininity

Enjoyable Sunday brunch on
the shared terrace.

What does a home built for women look like? How should the rooms function? What is the 'other', the feminine, which has not been considered until now? The 'ro*sa' society, the architect, Sabine Pollak and the real-estate developer GPA pursued these questions for nine years, until the women's building project became a reality. Now, three years after completion, Sibylle Hamann visited the house and its inhabitants for NiVo in order to write a report about community and community values.

Text: Sibylle Hamann
Photography: Katarina Šoškić

# Anyone

walking along Anton-Sattler-Gasse in the 22nd administrative district of Vienna who allows his eyes to run along the facades, cannot help confronting clichés in his own head. Perhaps there are more prams than usual in front? Or have the windowsills been decorated with an unusual quantity of lovely flowers? An apartment block for women could look exaggeratedly modest or exaggeratedly proud; especially conformist or especially avant-garde.

Then you stand in front of it. No, it is not coloured pink, even though it is called 'ro*sa'. The side facing the street has been kept in warm colours. Beige and dark-gray cement composite panels alternate with each other to look light, warm and yet tasteful as well.

'Ro*sa Donaustadt' is not an alternative commune. Neither is it a refuge, where mistreated women are protected. And, in spite of what wicked tongues may say, it is not a dangerous cave either, where men are eaten alive. This prototype project has forty apartments, of which two thirds have been leased to women from the society 'ro*sa Donaustadt'. To answer the most frequently asked question at once: yes, men may live in these apartments; as sons, friends, life companions. But as for signing the contract—they should rather leave that to a woman.

'Ro*sa Donaustadt' is not a privately funded luxury project but part of the publicly-supported Viennese building programme. This is intentional. For the women for whom it is designed are not among the privileged participants in the real-estate market. Most live alone, many are over sixty-years-old, some are solo parents. They may be an archaeologist or a book-keeper, a nurse or an artist there. Social housing does not mean that one lives with people of the same frame of mind, clinging on to each other. The remaining third of the apartments, consequently, is allocated by the housing service and according to its criteria; mainly to families with several children. People who often have no idea what they are getting into, which is usually not a problem, though sometimes can be.

"Oh yes, some meetings with people were strange," explained Mariana Potocnik, the former head of the society, one of the very first inhabitants, who has been living on the ground floor with her cat since December 2009, right next

to the notice board. She recalled a tenant sent by the housing service: "He was *such* a giant. He was always trying to assert himself against the women. But he soon left again," she said and couldn't repress a smile when she added the last sentence. Everyone gets along with the two Chinese families, a Philippine one and an extended family from India, who all came through the housing service.

Ms. Potocnik is 67 years old and a retired kindergarten teacher. All through her professional life she worked for social groups, and when she talks, attentively, animatedly and at the same time thoughtfully, it is clear that she has learnt to communicate.

> No, the building is not obvious from a distance. It is not in hiding, but neither does it challenge its surrounding. Anyone who does not want to know anything about it can leave this house undisturbed, or you have to come closer, get involved, if you want to find out what makes it special.

That was probably an advantage in the long, exciting, sometimes wearisome group-dynamic processes that have brought Ms. Potocnik to this point. For many years the group met every week or month to exchange ideas about feminist domestic utopias. The social conditions were discussed that hinder women from having a self-determined life. Outlines were drawn and discarded again, financial models worked out and debated, and people encouraged each other until this specific concrete house emerged from the abstract idea.

Ms. Potocnik has arrived, along with her cat. She conducts us through her 54-square-metre apartment with kitchen-cum-living room, small bedroom and bathroom. On her little terrace is a north sea beach basket-chair with a view of radiant sunflowers. The tightly calculated living area, she says, is "quite enough for a person like me." Especially since the space she lives is in reaches beyond the door of her apartement.

The pensioner, Mariana Potocnik, on the terrace of her ground-floor
apartment. The former club president is one of the initiators of the
'ro*sa' project and one of the very first inhabitants.

Alongside her apartment Ms. Potocnik also has the wide corridor, painted in a bright pea-green, the space is much more than just a connecting area between the various apartments. It has big windows with cushioned benches in the niches; there you can sit, gossip, read and watch the children play. Directly beside her apartment she has the big common room with a sofa, a table, a children's corner and a kitchen, where people can cook and eat together. Outside the kitchen there is a shared terrace, where someone makes a brunch on most summer Sundays. There is also a garden.

It often happens that Ms. Potocnik looks after the neighbours' children, when there is any need. She asks whether she should bring something for anyone else before she gets on her bike and rides down to the organic farmer's wife. Certainly, she has discovered that others do not always find it easy to accept assistance. Solo mothers, in particular, have learnt to fight their own battles. "But we can all learn together," she says.

Sabine Pollak conducts research and teaches at several universities. She has been working on feminism and domestic life as long as she can remember—both in theory and in practice. "The history of modern architecture can be read as a constant process of excluding women and femininity," she wrote in her book *Leere Räume. Weiblichkeit und Wohnen in der Moderne* (Empty Rooms. Feminity and Contemporary Living), which was published in 2004.

> This way of living does not come about by chance. There is an idea behind it. And an architect, who thought out the whole project and who realised it from the beginning.

Even while she was studying architecture, Sabine Pollak noticed a fundamental imbalance in domestic dwellings. On average, women spend far more time at home than men do. They also work substantially more in the house. But they normally have little to say when it comes to making contracts, planning and constructing apartment buildings. In the offices of the established property developers and in those of financiers and architects, women are just a tiny

The shared living room with sofa, table, children's corner and kitchen is frequently used, especially by the young inhabitants.

All generations live together in the women's apartment project, in various kinds of dwelling. In 2010 alone, eight babies were born in the building!

minority. Pollak is convinced that that can be clearly seen in the end product; the house.

She, herself experienced this deficit in person when she lived in a classic Viennese apartment building as the lone mother of a daughter. There was almost no contact with the neighbours. "There was the cliché bad-tempered house manageress, but nobody I could talk to," she remembers. This was also reflected in the architecture of the building. No room was available for meeting people. In such a setting neighbours can hardly be experienced as allies, but rather as disturbances: as rivals for the shortage of space, who block one's way with push-chairs or bicycles.

In modern social housing it was supposed to be quite different. Indeed the big community dwellings built by 'Red Vienna' between the Wars set new standards: suddenly there were green spaces between the big buildings, libraries, kindergartens and rooms for events, as well as laundries to be shared.

But the communal buildings still breathed the gender relationships of traditional small families. Every room had a clearly assigned purpose. This is where the parents slept, here the children were housed, the latter usually in narrow elongated rooms; and in between were narrow passages and many doors, so that all areas were kept firmly apart from each other. The kitchen was still merely a 'leftover room', usually with a view of the backyard and just big enough for one person to work alone, without troubling the other family members or guests with the sight, or worse still, with the clatter, of cooking pots.

Since then priorities have changed. The big combined cooking, dining and living room is now the norm in middle-class family homes. It is not only practical but also has good social value if you can watch the children from the corner of your eye while you are cooking. Whilst guests can give a hand with chopping vegetables. "Today, a big kitchen block in the middle of the room is considered smart, especially when men are standing at the stove," says Pollak.

Housework is not something you have to feel ashamed of and hide yourself when doing it. It is easier to bear when it can be visible, shared and performed in friendly places: it expresses a different, more modern idea of family.

One can develop this idea even further. Sabine Pollak conducts people through the building. Just how radically she has turned the conditions upside-down becomes

View from, and of, the building's roof terrace.

The side corridor is more than just a connecting area between the apartments. In the cushioned window niches, people sit down to talk, read and watch the children play.

clear when you reach the top floor. There, where the Penthouse is normally situated with a long-distance view over the roofs, is the laundry. The architect explains that, it was of course not at all easy to convince the financier that one could devote the most valuable square metres of a property to such a profane activity as washing clothes.

Only at a second glance does it look logical, for the wet sheets dry out far quicker up here than in a damp, dark basement. One can also bring the children with one, so that they can harvest tomatoes from the surrounding raised beds or nibble at strawberries. The sauna with a view is also far more attractive than the sauna at the back of the garage, where it is usually installed. Especially in winter, when you go outside after the sauna infusion, onto the snow on the flat roof with the city lights sparkling below.

The layout of the apartments also confronts the stubborn power of habit with a kind of architecture that puts women's needs at the centre. The everyday life and relationships of women are varied—in society in general as well as

in the case of the 'ro*sa' women. Some live with men, others with women; some with an intimate partner, others with people who are not so intimate, some with dependent children, others alone. In publicly-funded apartments all these realities are treated only as exceptions. There the norm is still the 70-square-metre standard apartment for the mother-father-child standard family.

Apartments that enable people to live self-determined lives have to be adapted to different versions of patchwork families and to the changing needs of their individual members. To make it possible for the widest range of uses, all rooms planned by Pollak for the 'ro*sa' house are neutral. You can join them together, or separate them, there could be room for a care-giver and when the daughter grows up she can have her own entrance.

In bureaucratic practice, however, the architect struck limitations. Several apartments were intended as shared flats; with individual bedrooms but a common dining area. At the last moment, however, intervening walls

The north-sea beach chair belonging to Mariana Potocnik, with a view of radiant sunflowers.

Liesl Fritsch, a retired pharmacist, attends to one of the circular flower and vegetable gardens on the roof terrace.

were installed, and small individual flats were created. It had been too difficult to work out the questions of liability in the contracts. Apart from that—the women who live there assume—the authorities probably did not quite believe in the long-term existence of the whole project and did not want to be left with unleasable apartments after the failure.

We looked into the library. It is a small apartment on the first floor, which the 'ro*sa' women also use as a club room. A portrait of Johanna Dohnal, the first Austrian Minister of Women's Affairs (1990) and an icon of the feminist movement, hangs on the wall. Liesl Fritsch, a retired pharmacist, is leafing through the volumes where everything has been archived: the minutes of the association's meetings, the debates with opponents and supporters and media reports. They had worked hard on the basic questions of human existence, on the line between individualism and solidarity and alternatives to capitalism, questions of power in society and personal states of being.

Many themes were thought about here. How to reproduce oneself without falling into the family trap; how the generation that invented the first shared apartments imagines life in old age; how private services could be shared if one did not want to be dependent on the state. "In many things we were ahead of our time," says Sabine Pollak; the city is simply not ready for many things.

However, the city is approaching. When you look down from the roof, you can see the cranes. In the spaces where a few years ago there were still workshops, garage repair shops and wild, undefined patches of green, today the Kagraner Spange is rising up, a big new residential area. Whether the rest of society wants it or not: 'ro*sa' is getting closer. In fact we are already almost in the midst of it.

The sofa corner in the common room;
popular with all generations.

Neighbourly communication is usually
informal in the 'ro*sa' building.

# Oblique conception

Δ developer brought ski tourism to the Rigi region in Switzerland; an architect designed sloping planes all his life. The holiday home Justus Dahinden erected on the Rigi, commissioned by his father, consists almost entirely of its pyramidal roof. To this day the house is regarded as one of the most extraordinary Eternit buildings in Switzerland, founding a career no less extraordinary, and giving the Zurich 'architect of slopes' an international reputation which contributed to his professorship in Vienna.

Text: Michael Hanak
Photography: Peter Tillessen

# Δt first glance the building looks like a single pyramidal roof. The architect calls it an "only-roof-house" and the owner calls it his "tent house". The small holiday home is on the southern slope of the Rigi, the 'Queen of Mountains'. Lonely and isolated, it is set apart from the rest of the village. There is a breathtaking view of a region in central Switzerland: across Lake Lucerne to the Urner Alps and the Obwaldner and Niwaldner Alps. The house itself is an eye-catcher as well—the crystalline form of the building is like an echo of the surrounding mountain peaks.

## Pyramid on the Mountain

The pyramid form leaning into the mountain rises above an almost square floor plan. The small building stands free of the ground as if on piles. The beams of the floor are held by four supports, which are cement tubes filled with concrete. The tapered house was erected entirely as a wooden construction. The slanted roof surfaces are clad with dark gray Eternit tiles, which are attached to a rear-ventilated slatted frame. Only the apex of the 'helmet' is made of metal.

The window apertures are cut out from the structure or set onto it as protruding dormers. On the south side, the facade is open along its entire width with a terrace recessed from the pyramid, which is protected by the roof eaves at the side. The two lateral surfaces of the roof have a wide dormer, the framework of which leans forward. The other windows on the north side lie on the same plane as the slanting roof.

From the porch, which one crosses to enter the house from the terrace, one comes into the central living room. Under the sloping roofs, bedrooms are arranged laterally, while the kitchen and bathroom lie on the side facing the mountain. Over the orthogonal main room, which is the only space surrounded entirely by vertical walls, there are other bedrooms, which can be reached via a steep staircase. Full use is made of the available space.

## Vision of a Ski Resort

The original client for the specially formed house on the alpine slope of the Rigi was Josef Dahinden. He was a descendent of the hotel dynasty, who once ran the Bellevue Hotel in Rigi-Kaltbad, which was later burnt to the ground. At the beginning of the 20th century, his mother started ski courses and initiated the first winter journeys on the Vitznau-Rigi railway. Thus the tourist mountain in central Switzerland became a pioneer site for winter sport. Josef Dahinden, himself, was a pioneer ski instructor. He published several books and films about skiing styles and is seen as the founder of rhythmic skiing. One of his many initiatives was to publish instructions for the 'Ski Mambo', which was further developed over time until it triumphed as 'kurzschwingen' and wedel ski techniques. He sang the praises of his mountain home as a "proud pyramid".

In 1954 the 'Rigian', now living in Zurich, commissioned his son, a recent graduate from the ETH, to build him a holiday home. It had to be situated directly next to the ski lift he had erected; which was later closed down due to lack of snow. The steam train that had connected Kaltbad to the Scheidegg had already been closed down in 1931. As a relic of that, there was an iron bridge below the house with two grilled pylons. The former railway line was used as an access path. Possibly, the owner was imagining a holiday village in this isolated spot. In any case he saw the projected holiday house as a prototype that might be copied.

## Architectural Universe on a Slant

The architect, Justus Dahinden of Zurich, drew up the plans for the holiday house including its furnishings. In fact he submitted several designs before his father was satisfied. It was his first project to be realised and marks the beginning of a remarkable career as an architect.

Born in 1925, after growing up in Zurich, Justus Dahinden became a student of architecture at the ETH Zurich. After graduation he worked as an assistant for Professor William Dunkel and wrote his dissertation 'Standortbestimmung der Gegenwartsarchitektur' (Strategic Analysis of Contemporary Architecture), for which he was awarded his doctorate. The Rigi House adorned the title page. In 1955, one year after it was completed, he opened his own architectural firm. Twenty years later he became a professor at the Vienna University of Technology.

His unconventional first work already has major elements of his later creations. Leaning facades and roofs are featured repeatedly in his work. A well-known example is the pyramidal Ferrohouse on the shores of the Zurich Lake (now the Pyramid Clinic at the Lake). Finally he transferred the slanting stack to the dimensions of urban design in the terraced City Hill project. Slanting spatial boundaries are intended to give inhabitants and visitors a feeling of security. "Tipping the facade into a slant lessens its threatening aspect and opens it up to the sky," Justus Dahinden wrote.

At the starting point of his designs are always 'humans and space' and the 'emotional efficiency' of the architecture. In his book of 2005, *Mensch und Raum,* he outlined the encounter of human with space.

This places Dahinden in a certain tradition of Modernism and ties him to Frank Lloyd Wright's call for a natural context and a humane form. With regard to symbolic content, he refers to Bruno Taut's unrestricted crystalline buildings and his Utopian 'alpine architecture' as well as Anthroposophic architecture, based on a holistic, spiritual view of the world.

As was the case in his first house, the form of the pyramid stood for the values Dahinden demanded of the buildings he designed. Since then the philosophy of the slope has accompanied his architectural universe, which has developed outside the mainstream. Today, the pyramid on the Rigi pays witness to the principle of searching for the new in post-war Modernism.

# After Nature

The brilliant craftsman and inventor Ludwig, Hatschek was searching for something industrial to work on. By a lucky chance he was able to buy a paper and cardboard mill in the Austrian town of Vöcklabruck in 1892. Hatscheck developed a vision of producing weatherproof roofing tiles instead of roof paper. After a series of failures and setbacks he discovered a "process for manufacturing paving slabs from fibre materials and hydraulic bonding agents". He was able to patent his discovery on 15 June 1901.

## 51 % PORTLAND CEMENT

This is made by firing chalk and clay. In particular the bonding of chalk and the silicic acid found in clay gives cement composite its considerable compression strength.

Photography: Cortis & Sonderegger
Text: Linus B. Fetz

As a qualified salesman, Ludwig Hatschek not only wanted to manufacture a mass industrial product cheaply; he also knew that a memorable name was needed for successful marketing. And so, on 19 September 1905 first generation Eternit was entered on the Austrian brand register. The logo, still used today with slight changes, was introduced by the Eternit factories in the 1930s.

## 2% REINFORCEMENT FIBRES

Those used were synthetic organic polyvinyl organic fibres (PVA). They are also used in the textile industry for clothing, protective materials, non-woven materials and medical sewing threads.

It is certain is that the resounding name 'Eternit' has achieved such a high level of recognition that the material is often named with that term. For example, we might read that building supplies companies have set up 'Eternit cutting centres', roofing and facade-building companies offer "Eternit facades" and garden centres sell 'Eternit vessels'. Even in essays on architecture, Eternit is often referred to as a building material, whilst art museums state that artists such as Cuno Amiet have painted with oil and tempera "on Eternit". To be accurate, however, 'cement composite' is, strictly speaking, the correct term for the product or material.

# 5% PROCESS FIBRES

These cellulose fibres prevent the cement-water-fibre mix from separating during the production process. For particular cement composite products one part of polyethylene fibres (PE) is added. As time progresses, the cellulose, which is only needed during production, dissolves. The hollow space that results is filled by the formation of crystalline hydration products in the cement. This leads to a durable increase in the strength of the product.

As its name suggests, cement composite is a compound material. Materials of this kind have been used by human beings ever since they first found ways to build and produce durable goods. To decrease the likelihood of breakage, the first potters mixed the mineral fibre asbestos into their clay pots. Nature produces composite materials far more successfully than humans can: plant stems have cellulose fibres arranged in parallel lines, which are embedded in the basic material of the cells. All composites have one thing in common: fibres from a wide range of sources reinforce the base material so that it can better withstand pressure.

## 12% WATER

In hardened cement composite only a very small amount of water is still present. It serves to further harden (hydrate) the cement matrix.

The process fibres supplied in the form of cardboard are enriched with water in the pulper, a huge mixing machine, separated into single fibres and further refined in a refiner. Until they are used for further processes, they are stored in huge wooden vats. Meanwhile the reinforcement fibres, delivered in bales, are mechanically loosened and the cement is well mixed in water. Finally, all these ingredients are measured into a big mixer and mixed with each other. This 'papier mâché' with cement as the binder is then ready for the production of the many kinds of cement composite products.

# 30% △IR

In cement composite this has the form of microscopically tiny pores. They serve as space for the expansion of freezing water, thus preventing frost damage. Due to this system of micropores, as in modern textile materials, a self-regulating, breathing and waterproof building material is produced.

# DETAILS
# 1 – 11

Architecture comes down to detailing. The following pages demonstrate this clearly. The projects presented here showcase an international selection of remarkable buildings that display an exemplary, constructive use of cement composite. For this industrially produced material opens up innumerable potential applications with its wide range of products and colours.

## HOUSE PLAK

Site: 1160 Vienna (AT) • Architects: propeller z, Vienna (AT) • Construction Period: 11/2009 – 5/2011 • Client: private • Roofing and Facade Contractors: MB Holz und Bau GmbH, Waidhofen • Cement Composite Panels: Eternit CARAT, ivory 7090

Clients, who are themselves part of the creative industry and have been looking forward for ages to the moment when the building is erected, are certainly not uncritical partners but rather partners who help to achieve a more precise result, after an appropriate phase of decision-making, many discussions and drafts. In the city, and yet in the green landscape, on a slope and with incredible views, a multi-storey building now shines in its white cladding with diagonal stripes.

### Próxima Estación: ¡Diagonal!

The announcement from Barcelona's public transport system buzzes incessantly in your ear in view of a building elegantly anchored to a slope in Vienna by the Austrian team of architects, propeller z. Even from a distance, the building stands out for its subtle patterning, produced by the way the facade has been covered with cement composite panels. The diagonal as an element of the design is continued inside the rooms. A stairway leads up from the street to a large-scale plateau, a kind of raised forecourt, roofed over by the projecting upper floors. Rounded recesses in the concrete are designed for plants. The generous scale of this area defines the atmosphere of the building as a whole. This entrance way makes it clear what has made propeller z famous: spatial quality, elegance and impressively but not ostentatiously, presented details (such as the structure of the hanging staircase to the upper floors).

### Athletic Angle

Inside, one can choose between ascending the hanging staircase or taking a lift that goes from the garage level up to the top floor; the bedroom level. Here the clients have not only realised a dream but also provided for the future. For, without a lift, hosting guests in the multi-storey building would definitely have been an athletic challenge. The five floors in turn were a response to making the best possible use of the hillside situation and to guaranteeing both a view and a high degree of privacy if the neighbouring plots are ever developed, or re-built. The clients went through a long search phase regarding both the building site and the selection of architects. Ultimately, Philipp Tschofen from propeller z was found to be the appropriate partner for discussions and decision-making processes.

### White Shawl

A wide range of variants were also considered for the wall cladding and many quotes were gathered—from Alucobond to plaster—many options were considered. The final decision—not least for reasons of cost—was to create Eternit walls. For when they had finally broken with their original idea of a metal shell—white was the defining choice of colour—and panels of the necessary quality were available in the form of Eternit. The walls were clad, and the qualities of this material were also applied to other purposes. For example, it was used both for window sills and the top rails of the balustrades, with a drip nozzle drilled into the plate.

The various levels and sequences of rooms are also determined by their various uses and orientations: the living area with the kitchen is designed as a split-level floor, with the living part generously oriented towards the city and a big terrace, while the slightly raised kitchen zone faces the hillside and the garden and has a small projecting balcony attached. Another of the levels, which relate to each other like open drawers, contains the library and workspace as well as a children's room. Sightlines throughout the whole building and the contrasts between white-clad walls and oak floors, doors and staircases, develop a skilful dramaturgy between views in and views out.

Text: Lilli Hollein

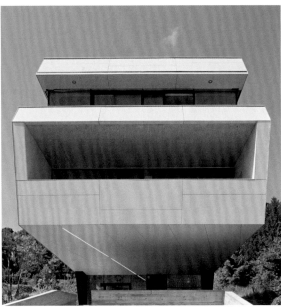

The five floors of the building resulted from the best possible use of the sloping the site and the assurance that there would be a view and a high level of privacy if anyone should build on the neighbouring sites.

Cement composite was used in various ways for its qualities. Apart from the wall it was also used for window sills and the upper part of the balustrades. The drip mould was milled into the plate.

# HOUSE PLAK

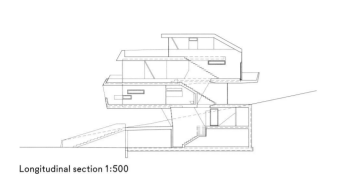

Longitudinal section 1:500

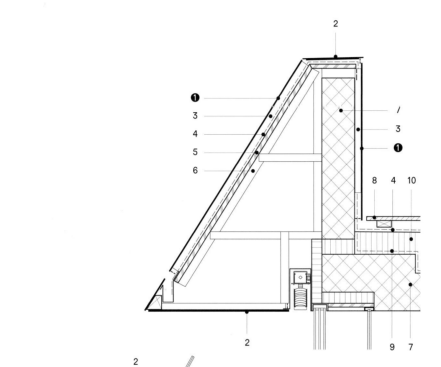

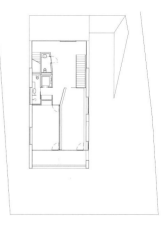

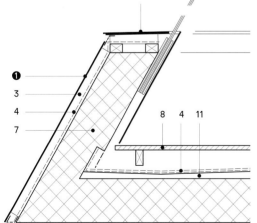

Vertical section 1:20

1   Cement composite panel 8 mm
2   Cement composite panel 12 mm
3   Rear ventilation
4   Roof insulation
5   Wood panel
6   Substructure
7   Concrete
8   Wood floor, exterior
9   Vapour barrier
10  Insulation
11  Screed to falls

4th floor plan 1:500

3rd floor plan 1:500

2nd floor plan 1:500

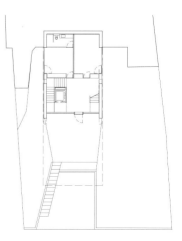

1st floor plan 1:500

## MULTI-FAMILY HOMES HOLLÄNDER

Site: Holländerstrasse 60–72, Uetikon am See (CH) • Architects: Wild Bär Heule, Zurich (CH) • Construction Period: 2007–2011 • Client: Hinderer Liegenschaften AG, Oetwil am See • Facade contractor: Gadola Fassaden AG, Oetwil am See • Cement Composite Panels: Eternit Ondapress 36, anthracite (vulcanit N 6512)

The northern shore of Lake Zurich is viewed as an affluent area. This is where the rich and the privileged have their homes. The lake and the slopes facing the evening sun have made this region a very popular place to live. However the residential construction firm of Holländer profits from these site benefits only to a certain degree. The architects of Wild Bär Heule have managed, nevertheless to create new benefits here.

### Creating Oases

While the neighbouring slopes provide a splendid panoramic view of Lake Zurich and the Alps, none of that applies to this particular building site. For one thing, it is situated on a small plateau on the slopes, and for another, a clump of trees blocks off the desirable view to the cresent-shaped water surface. But this place is by no means without its charm for all that, the architects believed: "We wanted to save as much as possible of the agricultural setting," Sabine Bär explains, pointing out the earlier purpose of the former cow pasture. Without a doubt, the conditions for that purpose existed at the edge of the settlement: the lot is lined on two sides with trees, higher on the

slope there are only a few scattered farm houses and a stream gurgles along the valley on the eastern boundary. The place was perfectly suited for realising the dream of building a home in a rural oasis. With this in mind, the architects designed seven compact multi-occupier houses, each with six large apartments. "Densify, certainly, but not with a brutal facade," was their motto. For this reason the buildings are set at angles to each other so that views can be glimpsed between them.

The architects also derived the facades of cement composite corrugated plates from the previous agricultural land-use: "The rural oasis," they wrote, "also finds its correspondence in the material qualities of the building shell." The rather rough haptic quality seemed to them to be a suitable reference to the closeness to nature they desired. But unlike farm sheds, where corrugated sheets are used in brown colours, for example in the neighbouring agricultural building, in this case an anthracite colour was used. In this way they make reference to the rural context while also going beyond it. By creating a balance between rural rawness and urban style, as expressed by the dark colouring as well as by the 'up-to-the-minute' floor plans and the high-quality interior cladding, the Wild Bär Heule team is perfectly in touch with the market. People who move to the country here are looking for "a rural oasis" while, at the same time, "not dispensing with proximity to the city," which is precisely what real estate marketers say. The architects respond to

these client wishes skillfully: their design combines well-versed market-oriented ideas of a sophisticated city lifestyle with the myth of country living.

### A Construction Challenge

At the same time, the architects followed unconventional paths. While the self-contained parts of the walls are covered with vertically oriented corrugated plates, so that the window sills and balconies form a horizontal band around the entire body of the building, thus creating an unusual horizontal montage. The different orientation of the corrugations is accentuated further because the horizontal bands project outward. In spite of this play of vertical and horizontal panel orientations, the buildings seem compact and contained within themselves. Apart from the materials used, this is also due to the fact that the construction volumes at the attic and ground floor levels have similar incisions. The architects had a hard construction challenge at the corner junctions of the buildings, where the horizontal corrugated plates converge. To make the corners sharp, they insisted that the cement composite panels be cut and attached in a mitred style. The facade contractor developed this unusual detail on the basis of a one-to-one model—the detail drawing was made subsequently for the present publication.

Text: KoRi

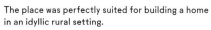

The place was perfectly suited for building a home in an idyllic rural setting.

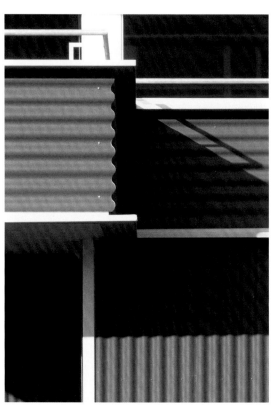

To form a sharp-edged corner, the cement composite tables were cut with a mitre.

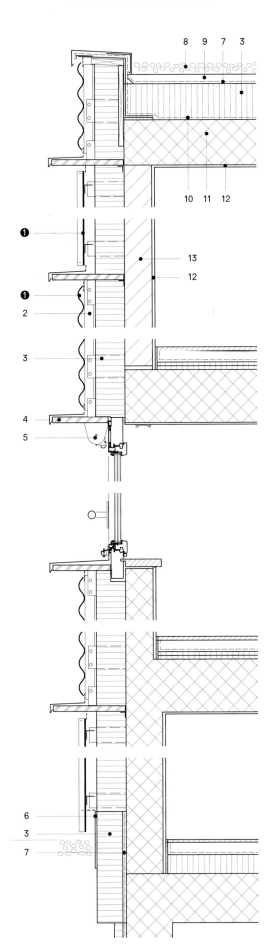

Ground floor plan 1:500

1 Cement composite panel 6 mm, corrugated,
  corners mitred
2 Rear ventilation, substructure
3 Insulation 160 mm
4 Brick wall, supporting, 150 mm
5 Interior plaster
6 Window ledge

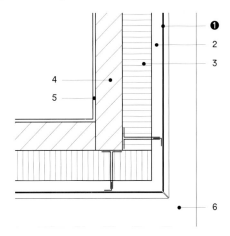

Plan junction corner 1:20

1 Cement composite panel 6 mm, corrugated
2 Rear ventilation, substructure
3 Insulation
4 Lintel element window and windowsill
5 Vertical awning, roller apron
6 Foundation sheet metal
7 Waterproofing
8 Gravel strip / extensive planting
9 Drainage mat
10 Vapour barrier
11 Concrete
12 Plaster
13 Structural brick wall

Vertical section 1:20

## DAYCARE NURSERY

Site: Geissbergstrasse 2, Ennetbaden (CH) • Architects: Rolf Meier Martin Leder, Baden (CH) • Construction Period: April–December 2010 • Client: Local Authority of Ennetbaden • Roofing Contractor: Neba-Therm AG, Olten • Cement Composite Panels: Eternit Integral Plan, Nobilis

'The Very Hungry Caterpillar' eats its way towards the town centre. The concept for the advertising project is also highly appropriate for the building itself: even the decision to use narrow, upright cement composite panels—selected for their durability—supports the caterpillar metaphor. As the panels cover all four outer walls and the roof, they translate the evenly sequenced segments of the 'caterpillar torso' into an architectural form. The all-enveloping facade becomes the caterpillar's clothing.

### David Eats Goliath

The arrangement of volumes in the structure also gives the new building "a playful appearance," write the architects, thus building an associative bridge to its intended use. The free-standing building sits directly on the ground—like the crawling creature used as a metaphor. The single-storey pavilion looks as though it were slowly creeping along—from Ennetbaden into the district capital. One might almost think that David is setting out to swallow Goliath. The 'creature' pushes its 'head' forward. Its lengthy body, with several twists, seems to be quite discreet and is yet clearly identifiable. At this point the variegated landscape of roofs reaches its highest point and a big opening looks out like an eye that is taking the measure of the approaching stranger. Initially, the 'animal' sustains its expectant poise and looks across to the authorities with its Cyclop's eye.

### Peristaltic Effect

The building's shell consists of weather boards on a pre-fabricated wooden frame, which greatly helped to reach the Minergie Eco standard for sustainable building. In terms of building technology, weather boarding has the advantage that it can easily be adapted to the relevant axial dimension, by having the panels overlap to varying degrees. The enveloping facade element also turned out to save materials because in each case it was possible to used the entire panel length of 2.5 metres; off-cuts were simply used on the next section. And not least, according to the architects, the weather boarding ensured a "lively surface structure", thus supporting, as does the building's volume, the apparent forward movement of the construction. The overlap of weather boards emphasises the longitudinal direction and thus the building's apparent forward thrust. The effect is enhanced by the fact that the direction of the panel-overlap changes when the building takes a bend as well as the rhythm of the roughly 40-metre long street front. The optical impression is reminiscent of the peristaltic movement of caterpillars.

The aesthetic and construction debate on the facade is matched by the artwork added by Fabia Zindel. Her small yellow plates of anodised aluminium decorate more than just the screws holding the cement composite elements as oversized washers. Because their diameter increases and decreases along the wall like a wave, the resulting grid of points also suggests a forward movement. The bright yellow of the disks makes them seem like small bright lamps on the otherwise yellow surface. This is repeated inside the building. Here yellow wardrobe furnishings also create a colour contrast in the otherwise monochrome interior: the floor is light beige throughout, the walls are clad with monochrome lasered three-layered panels, as is the ceiling in the reception area. The communal rooms have overlapping slats with acoustically determined gaps. The interior is like a colour-neutral stage for frolicking children, with brightly coloured toys and drawings on the walls.

Text: KoRi

# THE LITTLE BLACK HOUSE

Site: Gunskirchen (AT) • Architects: x architekten, Linz (AT) • Construction Period: 2009 – 2010 • Client: private • Roofing Contractor: Puschmann, Wels • Cement Composite Panels: Eternit Corrugated Sheet P6, dark gray

Setting of the rural space: graded rough asphalt, a small pond at the roadside, old fruit trees in the short cut grass, scattered farm buildings; behind them, fields, forests and bleating sheep. As natural as a small boulder that happens to be there, the house fits into the idyllic setting. Its lack of ostentation is due to a dark shell of corrugated cement composite panels on the roof and outside walls.

## Typology: Countryside

What makes a house recognisable as a 'house' is familiar from children's drawings: a few windows with four corners, a pitched roof with a chimney clear to see. A handful of such model elements combined with quotations from farmhouse typologies characteristic of the region have been reconstructed by X Architects into a new series of typologies. This story began with "a tight spatial plan and the willingness of the clients to tread an unconventional, even industrial path in construction style and materials." A dwelling place, openness to the surroundings, and work areas were to be understood—key word: farmhouse—as a combination of various functional areas under one roof. Thus the basic structure was designed as a main building and a secondary one with a covered yard between them. What resulted was a monolith in a wood-frame style. The only 'solid' parts are the floor slab of reinforced concrete and the rear-ventilated cement composite shell. Water simply flows away across the corrugated plates into the clipped eaves, devoid of pipes or gutters. Similarly reduced are the slim, framed square windows, which rest in the facade as though cut out with a sharp blade.

## A Picture of a House

The garden of the house is like a picture-frame for a painting of meadows, corn fields and hills. Anyone who comes into this development area with its picturesque backdrop can hear gravel crunching and smell wood and sawdust (which comes from the pellet-fuelled boiler in the house next door). On one side there are roughly sawn slats and roller gates with thin material above, on the underside of the ceiling. It is a white shed, an outside room to stroll through or to stop awhile—for the view and the garden, for the couple who own it and their guests, for birds, cats to enjoy and, of course, for the car.

## Not Every Monolith is Made of Stone

A simple pinewood pedestal takes you up one step into the main house. Now, at the latest, anyone who thought this was a monolith is in for a surprise. The room opens up wide and offers brightness and open living. The rural brief has been realised by subtle direction in a fresh manner. Nothing tips over into the rustic, not even the masses of wood on shelves and wall cladding. The white glaze on the Maritime Pine wall panels retains the cozy quality of the material and surpresses any urge one might have to yodel. The pale tones also place the outside colours even more emphatically into the picture—another way to frame the landscape. The two clients have made full use of this effect and have set fine accents in the green and yellow tones of the surroundings with furniture and accessories, which tie nature and house even more firmly together. The staircase fittings are of some scenic importance. It is almost surreal when one goes up into the bright light of the dome on the roof.

In its overall appearance, the house achieves what the 'Post-modernists' dreamed of: it speaks, and does so with multiple meanings. It is the stylisation of a house and yet also a built sculpture; in its materiality it narrates a raw industrial poetry as convincingly as its peasant prose, it creates abstract painting out of corrugations, joints and squares and simultaneously frames idyllic scenes of nature.

Text: Tobias Hagleitner

## HOUSE SCHLÜSSELHOFGASSE

Site: Steyr, Upper Austria (AT) • Architects: Kienesberger Schröckenfuchs, Linz (AT)
• Construction Period: 01/2009 – 07/2009 • Client: private • Holding Company:
Puschmann, Wels • Cement Composite Panels: Eternit CARAT, ivory 7090

Converting any historically listed building is a fundamental challenge for the planner and a risky financial venture for the client. Not only must the regulations governing historic monuments be respected, but the requirements for a 'modern' apartment must be set up in terms both of space and of energy technology. Many avoid the dangers by falling back on a new apartment in the city outskirts, and as a result many medieval houses are left empty, including those in the Upper Austrian town of Steyr. The Kienesberger Schröckenfuchs team of architects, acting as planners and clients in one, show what can be 'drawn out' of old building stock.

### Home in the City

The criteria for the new home of the Schröckenfuchs family were clear and ambitious from the beginning. The desire to live close to the centre and yet to have a large garden is an almost impossible ideal in a town like Steyr, both financially and architecturally. Thus a quick decision was made to adapt a run-down but centrally situated 16th century house.

### Structures from the 16th Century

Together with its four neighbouring buildings, the house forms part of a row of houses with a combined historic protection order, laid out not far behind the medieval city gate, along the Tabor Tower with a clear view of the river and townscape. The allocated space is built up along the narrow, elongated plot of land in a terraced manner, with the individual spaces connected by a continuous set of steps, stretching through the entire building to the hanging gardens. The private rooms are accommodated in the old tract of the building, which originally consisted of two structural sections and a small yard. The latter was taken over as an internal courtyard, with the bedrooms, bathroom and nursery arranged around it. The new extension is a bright, open unit of space making it possible to 'live right through' from the garden to the old town. The courtyard divides the space into an area adjacent to the garden, including a spacious open kitchen, and an area facing south, with the living room and a view over the old town and river. A continuous wall connects the rooms up to a height of 4.5 metres and is continued even outside on the terrace as a storage space for garden tools.

### Material Requirements

The service technology has also been made state-of-the-art and achieves a standard of 35 kWh/m$^2$ for minimum thermal heating requirements with a controlled air conditioning system. Additional energy is provided by solar panels, and a domestic water system reduces graywater consumption. Cement composite was used in several areas—both internal and external—because of its benefits in terms of materials technology. This material's resistance to moss, algae and weathering was especially beneficial in the shady courtyard and the north garden facade. Because of their large sizes, the panels could also be jointed with the extensive, floor-to-ceiling glass panels, concealing the uneven quality of the original facade. Covering the horizontal and vertical surfaces with only one material also results in a homogenous, seemingly monolithic surface. Cement composite was also used as a 'shower curtain' in the bathroom.

For the two architects, who founded their joint business in 2006, adapting the original substance was by far the greater challenge: "When building inside an existing structure one must be sensitive to the structure inherent in the building and then think from there. It is a kind of 'aha experience'—you realise why the houses were made as they are and why they work so well." The result also convinced the jury, who awarded the two young architects with the architectural prize for 'Best House 2011' in Upper Austria for their successful realisation of this planning challenge.

Text: Michael Hasslacher

# FAMILY HOME IN A FIELD

Site: La Tornalla 17, Villarepos (CH) • Architects: Aeby Aumann Emery, Fribourg (CH) • Construction Period: 2009 – 2010 • Client: private • Roofing Contractor: Gutknecht Holzbau AG, Murten • Cement Composite Panels: Eternit Ondapress, light gray (natural)

Two suspended concrete slabs, corrugated sheets of cement composite running right around and large openings: the elementary aesthetic of the building is closely associated with its materials and its manner of construction. This is illustrated, for example, in that the cement composite sheets used from stock defined the interior height of 2.5 metres. In other ways, too, the house gives witness to a pragmatic approach and an interest in high quality craftmanship for the details.

### Know-How

Aeby Aumann Emery Architectes were convinced that cement composite sheets could also be overlapped like weatherboard. It's just a matter of: how? In an initial test it was not possible to remove the formwork from the concrete once it had dried as it had not been sufficiently oiled. The two materials had stuck to one another and the formwork had broken. "In contrast to conventional formwork sheets, cement composite sheets are porous," explained the architect Patrick Aumann, "and that's why they have to be almost soaked in oil." The idea was tested immediately and proven to be successfull. The cement composite sheets could now be easily disconnected from the formwork and gave the concrete wall its characteristically corrugated form. However, the successful test was merely the beginning for other bespoke applications: having had no experience with the unconventional formwork material, the construction workers did not know how to work with it and so, in the end, the architects did the formwork application themselves over the weekend.

Why go to such lengths? "We wanted to connect the interior and exterior with each other," the architects explained, "not least in the choice of materials." For the outer walls they had already chosen corrugated sheets, to echo the neighbouring farm shed, which they had designed at the same time. They had also anchored this functional building in the rural context with the corrugations typical of agricultural buildings. In the case of the family home, the choice of material was intended to bring something from the surroundings inside. But using the sheets as cladding, as on the exterior, was not a viable option. For one thing, no secret was to be made of the structural function of the concrete walls. "And secondly, we didn't know, how the corrugated sheets designed for use outside would behave in the interior," maintained Aumann. For example, are they sufficiently heat-resistant to be used close to the fireplace? There was no experience to fall back on, and Aeby Aumann Emery Architectes did not want to take any unnecessary risks. Experimenting is fine, but not blindly: that is the core of their approach.

### Unrealised Ideas

This can also be seen in the fact that the architects had had other ideas, which they did not put into practice immediately. For example, they imagined corrugated cement composite sheets that could be slid and opened up. They also considered the option of perforating the panels. For the family home in Villarepos they tried out all the design options that could be supplied from the factory: it was possible to specify square-shaped punctures with rounded corners; there was even greater room for design variants in the fact that the gap between them and their location on the sheet can be altered. The architects used this for the bathrooms, the storage space and also in the corridor, where they wanted to have natural light but no windows visible from the outside. However, they haven't given up their earlier ideas completely. There may be another opportunity to use sliding window screens, Aumann revealed. In summer he intends to start another personal experiment. His goal: the ability to perforate cement composite sheets with even more freedom.

Text: KoRi

## LECTURE THEATRE WEICHENBAUHALLE

Site: Von Roll-Areal, Bern (CH) • Architects: Giuliani Hönger, Zurich (CH) • Construction Period: 2007 – 2010 • Client: Office for Plots and Buildings for the Canton of Bern (Amt für Grundstücke und Gebäude des Kantons Bern, AGG) • Roofing and Facade Contractor: GKP Fassadentechnik, Aadorf • Cement Composite Panels: Duripanel, light cement mixture, unfinished (lecture theatres), dark cement mixture (foyer), Duripanel, light cement mixture, finished (ancillary rooms)

Where the Swiss industrial enterprise, Von Roll once manufactured railway points from 1914, today students sit on study benches. For the architectural transformation, Giuliani Hönger referred to the house-in-a-house principle and designed two installations which affect the architecturally significant industrial wasteland as little as possible. Only in the roof area do the two 'houses' touch the existing outer shell, which it was possible to preserve almost totally. The roof superstructure was renewed according to today's standards and clad with cement composite corrugated plates, in order to preserve the character of the original.

### A House in the Building

The outer appearance of the Weichenbauhalle consequently remained unchanged, in stark contrast to its interior. There, two installed buildings with a total of seven lecture theatres ensure that the spatial effect is completely new. Between the brick shell of the existing hall and the facade of the installed buildings—due to deliberate measures—quite different interior spaces have resulted, to be used as foyer, relaxation and reception areas: while one of the lecture-theatre installations is oriented on the symmetrical axis of the hall, the other has been shifted from the centre. The spatial differentiation is enhanced by the fact that one of the buildings is aligned at ground-floor level, while the other is pulled back at the top like an attic floor. Furthermore, as one insertion cuts across the main direction of the hall and the other along it, spatial arrangements result that are reminiscent of urban spaces: narrow flights of rooms, high, vertical spaces as well as wide spaces resembling squares. A pattern of extended interlocking structures have replaced what was once a continuous large hall. The interior can no longer be grasped from one position but must be experienced by going through it. In connection with the new interior, the architects thus speak of 'alley spaces', which are adapted to various purposes on the model of urban planning. Even the artistic additions by the Chinese artist, Jun Yang, who lives in Vienna, aim at this kind of urban atmosphere: his red steel frames of various sizes and the fluorescent tubes inserted into them suggest neon advertisements of the kind found primarily in urban centres.

### Two Birds with One Stone

Between the lecture halls and the exterior wall there is not only a spatial transition area between the exterior public space and the academic surroundings of the lecture theatres, but also a thermal gap, since it acts as a climate buffer: on cold days the foyer can be heated up to a temperature of 15 degrees with the heat radiating from the buildings. To satisfy the high demand for energy, the installations and the roof were also provided with high quality insulation. The pre-fabricated wooden elements of the lecture theatres are covered with gray Duripanel tiles as a reminder of the hall's industrial past. For the foyer the architects chose a light gray finish and in the lecture theatres a dark gray one with a lighter cement mixture and acoustic perforations. The robust, untreated and uncut panels, which could be pre-fabricated in the factory and attached in a very short time, have a number of advantages: not only do they satisfy fire regulations, but because they are suitable for perforation it was possible to provide acoustically protected surfaces and ventilation gaps with the same kind of finish. Last but not least, they also meet the client's requirement to be able to remove construction elements with different life and usage times independently of each other (system separation). For example, the Duripanel elements can be simply unscrewed in order to perform maintenance work on the technical service components behind them. By using ecological materials, it was also possible to obtain the required 'Minergie Eco' certificate for long-term building.

Text: KoRi

## PAVILION AND AQUARIUM 'HUMAN FISH'

Site: Postojna Caves (SI) • Architects: Studio Stratum, Ljubljana (SI) • Construction Period: 2010 – 2011 • Client: Turizem Kras, d.d., Postojnska jama, d.d. • Facade Contractor: Demmo, Helbl Franc s.p., Laporje • Cement Composite Panels: SWISSPEARL® CARAT, Black Opal 7020 • Facade Material: SWISSPEARL® CARAT, Black Opal 7020

The caves of Postojna in Slowenia have a long tradition of visitors. Since as long ago as 1824, a fee has been charged for visitors entering the second-largest officially opened stalactite cave in the world. For that very reason its technical features have had to be constantly modernised. In 1884 the grottoes were equipped with electric light and in 1914 the petrol-driven tourist train started to operate. In 2010 an aquarium was built for a rare species of olm, whilst in 2011 it was extended with an exhibition and sales pavilion. Considering the humidity of almost 100%, it seemed logical for the architects of Studio Stratum to choose cement composite as the material for the facade.

### Precise and Durable

It was, however not only the constant humidity and a temperature of eight to ten degrees throughout the year that pointed towards the use of cement composite. Peter Šenk from Studio Stratum: "We were in search of an inorganic material that would not compete with the surrounding rock in colour or texture. Cement composite panels seemed logical to us under these specific conditions." Further advantages of cement composite for this unusual building site deep underground were that it is easy to cut and to process with precision, according to Šenk. In the end, all the building material had to be transported on the tourist train and assembled on site. Preparing in advance was only possible to a small degree. The entire basic structure of steel was mounted directly on the concrete base and covered with the panels cut into strips of equal size. Any slips in the manual work during assembly could be taken into account by the architects from the start and compensated for with the gaps between the narrow facade tiles. "Due to well detailed preparation, we were able to achieve the outside cladding that we wanted," Peter Šenk explained.

### A House for an Olm

The grottoes of Postojna are a popular place for an outing; in addition to visiting the limestone caves as a natural phenomenon, one can also attend dance evenings, concerts and other events. The first ball took place here in 1825, on a Whit Monday. But in the depths of the caves there are other interesting life forms: 84 different animal species adapted to life in caves—of which 36 are land-dwellers and 48 water creatures—live there far away from the streams of visitors. Only one of them, the roughly 30-centimeter-long grotto olm (*Proteus anguinus*), can be viewed in an aquarium by the almost 5000 visitors to the caves. Ideal conditions were to be created for both animals and humans. The pool stretches out towards the approaching visitors, thus creating a maximum window area for observation. The necessary technology for the extremely sensitive little creature with a life expectancy of at least 70 years (in natural surroundings) has been inserted in the narrow end piece of the aquarium. The roof is merely a metal grid, so that the dripping water can flow through.

### A House for Cavemen

A few metres further along the path, which is 20 kilometres in all, a huge hall opens up; it is mainly used for concerts because of its special acoustics. Along the stone wall, but without actually touching it, the pavilion was renovated and brought fully up to date technically by Studio Stratum one year after the aquarium was completed. The building was subject to the same conditions and requirements—and in addition a biological wastewater treatment system for the sanitation facilities was required. Cleverly, the architects put four entrances and exits into the transparent glass wall, so that, even here, freedom of movement was still guaranteed.

Text: MaHo

## APELVIKENS BEACH HUTS

Site: Varberg (SE) • Architects: Karlsson Wachenfeldt Arkitekter, Göteborg (SE)
• Construction Period: 2008 – 2010 • Client: Varbergs Fastighet AB (Building Department of Varberg City) • Roofing and Facade Contractor: Stiba AB, Borås • Cement Composite Panels: SWISSPEARL® CARAT Onyx 7090/7091/7099, SWISSPEARL® PLANEA Onyx 7090-R Colour

Although the stretch of coast around Varberg in southern Sweden is picturesque and its sandy beaches are very popular, during the colder time of year, the gales pound in, sometimes relentlessly, from the sea. This creates special conditions for local architecture. Wind, sand, salt and sun demand an especially resilient exterior for buildings.

### Salt and Sand Winds

During the warmer months, crowds of tourists stream into Varberg, which has a long tradition as a summer resort. This coastal town has made a widespread reputation for itself among sun worshippers, bathing beauties and surfers. Over the weekend the sandy beaches attract short-term holidaymakers from the interior of the country. One of the destinations is the 'Apelviken Strand', the beach where the local tourist office erected a holiday village with 32 bungalows. Throughout, two units at slight angles to each other are grouped into four rows. Following the principle of beach chairs closed on three sides, in each case only one side of a house is open. On the sites directly facing the beach, the cottages are not oriented towards the sea, as one might think, but towards each other in two rows. In other places, as many apartments as possible might be granted a view, however small, to the water, but here they are turned towards each other. You might think that this is an expression of community spirit, but it also has a practical reason: the number of open facades exposed to the weather can be minimised, which, with all the winds bearing salt and sand, considerably extends their lifetime.

### Subtle Shades of Gray

The exterior walls of the double cottages are consequently quite different from one another. While the inviting front aspect with the entrance and a sitting area has generous amounts of glass, the other three facades have no openings for windows, or minimal ones at most. The weather-dependent wall design expresses itself in the choice of materials as well: the entrance fronts have wooden slats, but the rear and side walls, like the gable roofs, are completely covered with indestructible cement composite panels. These are attached to a substructure of wood. Thus, four out of five sides of the buildings are durably protected from external weathering effects, as numerous other cement composite applications close to the sea confirm. The material also withstands sea winds, which carry salt and sand particles. But more than this convinced the client and the architects: "The choice of cement composite panels also provided the basis for an aesthetically convincing appearance," the architect Johan von Wachenfeldt explained. A homogeneous optical impression was important for him, and yet a monotonous holiday village was also to be avoided. Consequently the beach cottages differ from each other very little in colour, contrary to the first impression. This was possible because of the wide range of colours, including more than 30 different shades. "And so we were able to select three different shades of gray and not disturb the uniformity of appearance in spite of these subtle variations," the architect concluded.

Text: KoRi

## GIANT INTERACTIVE GROUP HEADQUARTERS

Site: Husong Highway, Shanghai (CN) • Architects: Morphosis, Culver City (US) • Construction Period: 2006 – 2010 • Client: Giant Interactive Group, Shanghai • Roofing and Facade Contractor: Beijing Jianghe Curtain Wall Co., Ltd., Shanghai • Cement Composite Panels: SWISSPEARL® XPRESSIV, Dark Gray 8220 (Facade), SWISSPEARL® CARAT, Anthracite 7020-R (roof), SWISSPEARL® CARAT, Onyx 7099 (interior)

The clients call their new Corporate Office Building in Shanghai a 'dragon' which is certainly a positive term in China, where the dragon is seen as a bringer of good fortune and a symbol of power. It is impossible to imagine any more appropriate metaphor than this fire-breathing creature for the building that rises from the earth and winds its way through fields and water. The 'dragon's skin' is a shell of cement composite panels that fulfils the wish for flexibility and all formal items on the facade, the roof and the interior.

### A Building Landscape

The master plan from the landscape designers, SWA for the area in the satellite town of Songjiang was not quite finished when Morphosis started planning the headquarters of the Giant Interactive Group. There and then a joint effort was started on conceptual work and a blend of building and landscape was developed. Morphosis designed a two-part building landscape, 75% of which digs itself under the ground—inspired by the original conditions of the site, a region of swamps and agriculture with irrigation canals. As if one had pulled and shaken something at the edge of the field, the building forms waves in a grand gesture under a huge green roof. A constructed dragon, that twists, winds, rises and sinks on the 3.2 hectare site until it stretches its 30-metre-long head out over the artificial lake.

In contrast to the dense city centre of Shanghai, 30 kilometres away, Morphosis found "space and free room" here. Apart from the maximum height and a deliberately light building density, the architects faced no restrictions. The comprehensive programme for the area was, however, implemented structurally and by no means superficially. Paths, squares, offices, or open spaces, roof, swimming pool: no clear hierarchy or rigid order can be found in the structure. The spaces seem to 'come about' somehow. Yet this lightness and openness is based on strict geometric principles—made possible by a heavy steel frame and a system of interior supports which are independent from it. This constructed flexibility goes right through from the space requirements to the way the building site is organised.

### Facade Space

Cement composite has been used for Morphosis projects, quite often before. However never so comprehensively as in the headquarters in Shanghai. There are several reasons for this. On the one hand, it was clear to the architects that such a complex structure required material that could be easily worked on site, and this, considering the size of the building site, also saved on material and resources. On the other hand, the architects wanted walls, which, in contrast to some alternative metal panels, as long as would retain their colour and haptic qualities for 20 or 30 years, and which, in addition, could be perceived as a homogeneous shell. Considering these parameters, the choice of cement composite was logical. A further advantage was that China has one of the best and most modern steel-processing industries, so that Morphosis was able to design the underlying construction of the double facade precisely according to 3-D models. The cement composite panels are attached with a relatively large, 800-millimeter gap from the construction. In this layer all necessary technology is housed—and concealed.

### The Big Picture

In the interior, the spatial play with landscape is continued, though, in this case artificially. The design of each individual area is different according to its function, though every room enjoys natural light and views. Many are clad with cement composite. The building is composed of a western and an eastern section divided by an approach road. All public rooms are in the western tract under the green roof, while the offices and infrastructure facilities face east towards the lake. The overall picture presents itself as a self-contained village for the Giant Interactive Group.

Text: MaHo

## WOMEN'S HOME PROJECT RO*SA DONAUSTADT

Site: 1220 Vienna (AT) • Architects: Koeb & Pollak, Vienna (AT) • Construction Period: 2008 – 2009 • Client: WBV-GPA Residential Association for Private Employees • Facade Contractor: DYWIDAG GmbH • Cement Composite Panels: Eternit PLANEA Special Colours

Something special, and yet fitting, both sophisticated and integrated: this building with high socio-economic requirements for its inhabitants presents itself as full of contrasts. It is integrated into a suburban conglomerate of terraced houses and 1960s-style high-rise blocks—and distinguishes itself from all that even with its front elevation.

### Experimental Women's Housing Project

The architects Koeb & Pollak allocate their prototype for a female target group to the tradition of Red Vienna. The development was carried out in joint planning with the 'ro*sa' association, whose own initiative accompanied it from the first idea to the search for a site and a client/sponsor. The model was eventually realised almost nine years later in a long, narrow building site in the 22nd administrative district of Vienna. The building makes use of the entire area available for construction; the maximum cubic space is reduced to the prescribed 70 % with gaps incorporated into the structure. This gives the elongated building its rhythm, which is increased even further by the facade with its colour contrasts.

### Strong Construction for Flexibility

To satisfy the wish for variable ground plans and apartment sizes, the architects chose a system of slabs and supports in reinforced concrete. In this way it was possible to solve the construction with supports and ceilings, apart from a very few slabs in the longitudinal and transverse directions. To avoid a district heating pipe running on the site and yet to set the building to the edge, it projects as a cantilever from the ground floor. The structural panels and supports are consequently set at a distance from the facade, which clearly reinforces the impression of openness and permeability in the interior of the building. In all the apartment types, the structural elements are separate from the room-defining elements, merged into columns, thus enabling even later adaptations and changes to the ground plans. In addition, larger apartments have a planned breakthrough point for a second entrance, so that they can be subdivided at a later stage.

### In 'Viennese Style'

The decision in favour of cement composite panels was made relatively early, after the design committee had rejected the original plan for fully insulated walls. The original plan was for black, but Koeb & Pollak chose a more playful two-colour solution. Thus the entire facade of the building, including the loggias, is clad with large-format, vertical panels in the subtle colours of beige and dark gray. The panels were laid in 'Viennese Style', which simply means that 'hindrances' such as wall projections or openings for windows are not included, but rather the panels are trimmed in front of them and a new section is made after them. "The facade of the women's home project is a variation of this 'Viennese Style'," Sabine Pollak explains. If an incision was necessary because of a window opening, the colour was changed and individual panels were emphasised with the contrasting colour. Uniformity was undermined—in spite of the uniform panels and window openings of the same size; what resulted was a beige-gray play with shades, which allows the facade to have a rather sculptural appearance.

The inverse of the void to the body of the building is the passage on the inside. A space that would normally be called a corridor. In the case of 'ro*sa' the passage takes the form of an incision along the entire length of the building structure, an internal three-storey-high circulation space three metres in width. With varying heights of the space, niches and lighting effects, the passage becomes a semi-public zone and quite often an extension of the living rooms—especially for the children of the house.

Text: MaHo

## DESIGN
Kitchen unit *Camouflage*

The kitchen unit has become indispensible as a central design element in modern living spaces—but until now cement composite has not been used for this purpose. The *Camouflage* design by destilat, a block with cement composite cladding, is a thematic and optical reminder of its traditional use for exterior wall shingles, but has a far more dynamic and individual pattern of alignment, because the kitchen unit should be different for each project—including the colour.

Design: destilat (AT)
Showroom destilat
Lehárgasse 10, 1060 Vienna
www.destilat.at

## EXHIBITION
*Wild Club*
→ page 32

The 'Wild Club' was founded in 2008 by the French architect, Vladimir Doray. Every month Doray sends a picture of a 'site' to about 1000 members. The project proposals have to be sent back within 24 hours. The exhibition in the Paris Pavillon de l'Arsenal in spring 2010 documented these ideas, illustrations and drawings up to and including fully composed designs and wild project proposals.

272 pages, 11 × 17 cm
260 illustrations
www.wildclub.be
www.pavillon-arsenal.com

## FILM
*David. E la nave va*
In memory of David Sarkisyan

The film is a homage to the life and creativity of David Sarkisyan, who was director of Moscow's museum of architecture, MUAR from 2000 to his death in 2010. Many of his associates, friends and architects, such as Eugene Asse, Juri Grigoryan and Alexander Brodsky, have their say and describe the remarkable, charismatic David and his own rather eccentric museum world.

Director: Oleg Bermanas
Editor: Irina Bakhtina
www.david-memory.com

## PUBLICATION
Bathing Pleasures – A Journey to the Most Unusual Baths in Central Europe by Iris Meder

Iris Meder, art historian and a profound expert on modern architecture in Central Europe, visited Central European swimming pools and thermal baths and collected the gems of both historical and contemporary bathing culture in her book. Functions range from Turkish baths, built over thermal springs in Hungary in the 16th century, through public baths to military swimming schools—an important building genre in the 19th century, usually built beside lakes or rivers—which were opened to the public around 1900.

Photo: Rudas Thermal Bath, Budapest

*Badefreuden – Eine Reise zu den aussergewöhnlichsten Bädern in Mitteleuropa*
192 pages, 16.5 × 21 cm
colour prints throughout, bound with dust jacket
EUR 25.–
www.metroverlag.at

## DESIGN
*Cemlight* by Rainer Mutsch

During a workshop at Eternit Austria in August 2011, the prototype of an outdoor lamp was developed from single cement composite bowls in cooperation with the Studio Rainer Mutsch. Completely at home with the material, as the designer of the outdoor furniture system *Dune*, Mutsch developed a limited series of pendant luminaires from three bowls using hand-formed cement composite. The bowls are connected with a fluorescent cable. *The Imperfect* with its rough surface is not yet in production …

www.rainermutsch.net

## INSIDE
The Cement Composite Wet Cell

Large-format cement composite panels were used for this shower. Prefabricated sections were simply mounted with building adhesives directly onto the rough coat as a wet cell inside the wet cell. Also important is the (almost) seamless optical impression. Impregnation with furniture wax renders the panels water-resistant.

Planning: DI Ralph Broger, Bezau
www.eternit.at

## FOUND ITEM
*Boulder*
Design by Michael Bruggmann
Photography: Michael Lio
→ in the next issue, NiVo 2

Design is invisible according to the architect Laurids Ortner. For the seat object *Boulder* by the designer, Michael Bruggman, this is completely accurate—the 'erratic block' must first be found in an open area. Although it is no longer on the list for delivery, we 'found' it worthwhile to present it.

Size: L 130 cm × W 100 cm
Height: 55 cm
Weight: 40 kg
Colour: gray

## A DAY IN THE LIFE OF …
Stéphanie Gygax photographed by Anders Holte
→ page 3

The photographer, Stéphanie Gygax, accompanied the CEO of FibreCem, Anders Holte, for two days on his travels, at his factory visits, meetings and discussions. We will present the series of photographs in the editorial of our next issues. Here is a mirror-view of Gygax by Anders Holte.

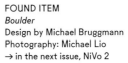

## PUBLICATION
*As Long as It Photographs*
*It Must Be a Camera*
by Taiyo Onorato & Nico Krebs
→ page 20

In two large-format magazines, published by the authors themselves, the two Swiss artists, Taiyo Onorato & Nico Krebs, present their latest photographic and conceptual works. The camera as object and the photographer as subject are given ironic roles.

60 pages, 29.7 × 42 cm
Colour and black-and-white offset
EUR 25.– (+ shipping)
Orders: order@tonk.ch
Preview: www.tonk.ch

1

3

8

6

5

2

7

**1  Aeby Aumann Emery Architectes**
(b. 1972, 1970, 1969) first met at the
Fribourg College of Engineering
and Architecture, where they have
been working together since 2006.
Before that the three young architects had accumulated a wide range
of experience at home and abroad
in the first ten years of their professional activities. They benefit from
that today. The works of Aeby
Aumann Emery pay witness to the
skilful and broad architectural background of its partners.
www.aae-architectes.ch

**2  Iwan Baan** (b. 1975) proposed to
Rem Koolhaas an interactive website
for his Europan project in 2005—
and in this way received his first
commission for architectural photography. Since then Baan has been
taking photographs for all the top
architects in the world, such as
Herzog & de Meuron, Thom Mayne
and SANAA. International journals
of architecture publish both his
contemporary and his historic essays
on architecture. In addition to
numerous publications in magazines and monographs, he still finds
time for his independent publications, such as *Brasilia – Chandigarh
Living with Modernity*. www.iwan.com

**3  Jojakim Cortis** (b. 1978) and
**Adrian Sonderegger** (b. 1980)
began working together in 2005
while studying photography at the
HGKZ (School of Art and Design
Zurich, now ZHdK), where they
have been teaching since 2009 and
2010 respectively. Their complex
productions are to be found both in
the editorial field and in advertising.
For NiVo they set the components
of cement composite into context
for the Eternit-Werk Niederurnen
under the heading 'Insights'.

**4  Linus B. Fetz** (b. 1939) is a civil
engineer (ETH/SIA). Between 1964
and 1970 he was on the scientific
staff in the Earthworks Department
of the Versuchsanstalt für Wasser-
bau und Erdbau (Research Institute for Hydraulics and Earthworks) at the ETH Zurich. He then
worked until 1986 as a research engineer and Director of the Central
Laboratory at Betonstrassen AG. In
1983 he directed the postgraduate
course 'On Soil-Cement' at the Es-
cola Politécnica da Universidade de
São Paulo, Brazil. From 1986 to
2001 he was Director of Marketing
and the Environment at Eternit AG,
Switzerland.

**5  Gina Folly** (b. 1983) lives and
works in Zurich and Basel. Since
2005 she has been working as a freelance photographer. She has carried
out commissions, for example, for
*Das Magazin, Art Collector, hochparterre*
and the architects Herzog &
de Meuron. Gina Folly has concentrated on making material visible in
her artistic work. Her works have
already been presented in a range of
exhibitions, such as *Idea Fixa No.1*
2010 at the Zürich Hochschule der
Künste, where she has also been
studying since 2011.
www.ginafolly.ch

**6  Lorenzo Giuliani** (b. 1962) and
**Christian Hönger** (b. 1959) have
been running their own firm in
Zurich since 1991. They have made a
name for themselves since then with
their regular successes in competitions. One of their key projects is
the Fachhochschule Sihlhof in Zurich
(2000 – 2003), which won several
prizes for architecture and is known
outside Switzerland. Several major
projects such as the Fachhochschul-
zentrum in St. Gallen (2003 – 2012)
and a home for the aged in a Zurich
suburb (2007 – 2011) are currently
being realised.
www.giulianihoenger.ch

**7  Stéphanie Gygax** (b. 1975)
studied photography at the Ecole
d'Arts Appliqués, Vevey, in French-
speaking Switzerland. She works
as a photographer on commission
for practically the entire magazine
industry in Switzerland. In addition
to a large number of solo and group
exhibitions and publications, in
2010 she brought out a monograph
with the photographs of her grand-
father Jean-Paul Chatelanat. In
2001 she was awarded the Swiss
Design Prize. Since 2003 she has
also been teaching at the Geneva
University for Art and Design.
www.stigy.net

**8  Tobias Hagleitner** (b. 1981)
studied architecture at the Art University in Linz and since 2008 has
been working as curator, writer, and
researcher at the interface between
art and architecture. Apart from
various periods abroad, in South
Africa and Bangladesh, Hagleitner
has worked primarily in Austria. In
2011 he received a PhD grant in
Urban Studies and Media Theory at
the Art University in Linz.

**9**

**11**

**13**

**12**

**10**

**15**

**9  Michael Hanak** (b. 1968) is an art and architecture historian in Zurich and works as an agent for architecture. He edited the book *Nachkriegsmoderne Schweiz* (Birkhäuser Verlag, 2001) with Walter Zschokke on the occasion of the exhibition of the same name (Vienna, Basel, Zurich). From 2004 to 2011 he was editor-in-chief of the Eternit magazine *ARCH*. He went to see the Rigihouse built by Justus Dahinden for NiVo.

**10  Sibylle Hamann** (b. 1966) is an Austrian journalist, political scientist, university lecturer, and author. She is a regular columnist for the daily *Die Presse*, journalist for the Viennese weekly *Falter*, and in 2008 (together with Eva Linsinger) she published the book *Weissbuch Frauen, Schwarzbuch Männer: Warum wir einen neuen Geschlechtervertrag brauchen*. Sibylle Hamann wrote a report on the women's home project 'ro*sa' and its inhabitants for NiVo.

**11  Lilli Hollein** (b. 1972) studied Industrial Design at the University of Applied Art in Vienna and since 1996 she has been working mainly as a curator and journalist for daily newspapers, magazines and, for example, the cultural section of Austrian Television (ORF). In 2007 she was appointed as curator of the Austrian contribution to the 7th Architecture Biennale in São Paulo. Together with Tulga Beyerle and Thomas Geisler she founded the 'Special Interest Group Design', whose activities have included calling the Vienna Design Week into existence in 2009, and whose directors are Lilli Hollein and Tulga Beyerle.

**12  Tibor Joanelly** (b. 1967) is an editor at *werk, bauen + wohnen*. After graduating in architecture from the ETH Zurich in 1993 he worked at first as an independent architect and for various firms. After teaching as an assistant at the ETH Zurich he became a lecturer for building design and structure and for architectural theory at the University of Liechtenstein. He has lectured in architectural theory at the Zurich University of Applied Sciences (ZHAW) since 2007.

**13  Karlsson Wachenfeldt Arkitekter** were fortunate: their workshop is located in the former Swedish Film Institute in Göteborg. The impressive building with patina has a lot more years of history than the office founded by Mattias Karlsson and Johan von Wachenfeldt in 2005. They recently opened a restaurant with their ten members of staff and are currently working on a passive house and a shopping centre. www.kawarkitekter.se

**14  Kienesberger Schröckenfuchs Architekten** insist on their rather 'unwieldy' corporate name. The two architects Marco Kienesberger (b. 1974) and Michael Schröckenfuchs (b. 1975) met one another at the engineering school (TU) in Graz and, after working in various architectural offices, they decided to found their own together in Linz. Since then a wide range of projects and building types has accumulated. In 2010 a branch was opened in Wels. www.kiesch.at

**15  Koeb & Pollak Architektur** is the corporate name for Roland Koeb (b. 1955) and Sabine Pollak (b. 1960). They have been planning, researching and teaching together in the fields of residential building and residential theory, office and industrial building and urban and gender research since 1995. In 2008 Sabine Pollak became Director of the Department of Architecture and Urban Studies at the Art University in Linz. In addition to the women's apartment building 'ro*sa' (2009), they have also realised the Therapeutic Commune in Ebenfurth (2006), Supervised Living in Spillern (2011), and the residential building BOA in OASE 22 in Vienna Stadlau together with Alexander Achmoeger.

16

17

20

22

23

19

21

**16 Rolf Meier** (b.1968) and **Martin Leder** (b.1973) have been running a joint business in Baden in the Canton of Aargau for almost a year. During that time they have made a name for themselves with their competition successes. One of their key projects is the new office building for the electricity concern Axpo in Baden, completed in 2010 and already the recipient of several awards. Very recently, the book *Anthologie 20* about their work to-date was published by Quart Verlag in Lucerne. www.meierleder.ch

**17 Xavier Mora** (b.1982) has been taking photographs since he was fifteen years old. His artistic works as 'Monsieur Xavier' often tell surrealist stories. He also loves to play with the materials, manipulating them and experimenting, for example, with development processes in the laboratory. In 2010 his work could be seen at the Biennale photographique d'Aramon and in *Révélation,* the show for contemporary photography in Paris. Mora is a Master of Arts (Sorbonne, Paris) and an artist for the Galerie VOZ'Image (boulogne-Billancourt). www.monsieurxavier.com

**18 Morphosis Architects** was founded in 1972. For thirty years the name has indicated the design director and Pritzker prize-winner (2005) Thom Mayne (b.1944). In his offices in California and New York, about 50 architects and designers work on international projects, such as the Giant Headquarter realised in Shanghai in 2010. The Phare Tower should be completed in the prominent La Défense, Paris, in 2015. www.morphosis.com

**19 Taiyo Onorato** (b.1979) & **Nico Krebs** (b.1979) both studied photography at the Art University in Zurich. Since 2003 they have been working together as an artist duo resident in Zurich and Berlin. After many solo exhibitions, such as those in the MoMA, New York (2006) and the Fotomuseum Winterthur (2010), the Kunsthalle Mainz instituted a comprehensive retrospective of the two artists for the first time in 2011. Taiyo Onorato & Nico Krebs created a Carte blanche with the installation-analog photo-work *Constructions* for NiVo. www.tonk.ch

**20 Radim Peško** (b.1976) Studied at the Art Academy in Prague and in London; in 2004 he graduated from the Werkplaats Typografie. Radim Peško lives in Amsterdam as a graphic designer; his main focal points are typography and font design. He works regularly for various publications, including *Dot Dot Dot Magazine.* He is currently teaching at the Rietveld Academie in Amsterdam. For NiVo he created the font *Fugue (Nivo # 1),* which will be further developed or will evolve for each new issue. www.radimpesko.com

**21 Propeller z** refers to Korkut Akkalay (b.1965), kabru (b.1966), Philipp Tschofen (b.1968) and Carmen Wiederin (b.1964). Since 1994 propeller z has been creating a broad œuvre of projects in the fields of architecture, interior design and exhibition design. At first known especially for various exhibition projects, they have attracted attention in recent years by realising three vineyards. In 2010 one of them, Weingut Claus Preisinger, won the Austrian Architectural Commissioners' Prize. www.propellerz.at

**22 Reiner Riedler** (b.1968) is self-taught. At the centre of his photography is the human being and the environment. For his documentations like *Albanien, Leben an der Peripherie* (2001), *Ukraine. Fotografien* (2003) and *Fake Holidays* (2009) he has set himself as traveller and researcher right inside the living spaces—looking for longings and voids. His artistic photographs have been exhibited, for example, in the Centre Pompidou, Paris, and the Kunsthalle Schirn, Frankfurt. Furthermore he has a great website address: www.photography.at

**23 Luca Schenardi** (b.1978) is an illustrator and artist based in Lucerne. He studied at the University for Design in Lucerne; since 2003 his illustrations appear regularly in many Swiss newspapers and magazines. His book *An Vogelhäusern mangelt es jedoch nicht* (working title) will be published in spring 2012 by the publisher Edition Patrick Frey. In the current issue of NiVo, Luca Schenardi illustrated the column R.S.V.P. www.lucaschenardi.ch

24

28

26

25

27

29

**24 Katarina Šoškić** (b.1983) is a Serb artist and photographer. She studied at the College of Applied Art in Belgrade, where her graduation work was *rb-61/120* (120 photos of views of her neighbours' terraces). Since 2008 she has been studying at the University of Applied Art in Vienna. Her photographic works have been published, for example, in the magazines *vice* and *Avenue Journal*. Katarina Šoškić portrayed the inhabitants of the women's living project 'ro*sa' for NiVo. www.katarinasoskic.net

**25 Dietmar Steiner** (b.1951) has been Director of the Architecture Centre Vienna since 1993, and in 2002 he was head of the committee for the Austrian contribution to the 8th Architecture Biennale in Venice. Among other positions, Steiner is a member of the Steering and Advisory Committee for the European Union Prize for Contemporary Architecture—Mies van der Rohe Award, President of ICAM— International Confederation of Architectural Museums, and chairman of the Quality Committee for social building in Vienna. In addition, Dietmar Steiner is well known for his lively public activity relating to the themes of architecture and urban development.

**26 Studio Stratum** was founded in 2003 by Polona Filipič and Peter Šenk. Both graduated from Ljubljana University in the Faculty for Architecture, supplemented with the Master of Excellence (2003) at the Berlage Institute in Rotterdam. In addition to architecture, research work is an important activity for both business partners. In addition to their teaching activities, both work for various organisations: Polona Filipič for Architecture and Children, and Peter Šenk as founder of the Institute for the Politics of Space. www.studiostratum.net

**27 Peter Tillessen** (b.1969) studied photography in Prague and Zurich and now lives as a freelance photographer in Zurich. Tillessen created photo-essays and picture stories on various editorial topics for magazines like *Du, Das Magazin,* and *Brand eins.* Other focuses: architecture and corporate photography. His artistic works have been seen in exhibitions and books like *Gold* (2001), *The Language of Humor* (2008), and *Oil* (2010). www.tillessen.com

**28 Wild Bär Heule** have been working together in this constellation since 2004. Previously Sabine Bär (b.1958) and Thomas Wild (b.1958), who graduated in architecture from the Engineering University Stuttgart in 1986, had already made two dozen residential buildings in the Zurich area. Since the ETH graduate Ivar Heule (b.1970) has joined them as a partner, they have confirmed their reputation for architecture that is both pragmatic and sophisticated. Many architecture prizes, including Best Architects 12, have impressively underscored this. wbh-architekten.ch

**29 x architekten** is a joint operation of architects with offices in Linz and Vienna, which reforms itself from project to project. The idea: a team without a hierarchy rather than the professional image of architects as lonely fighters. The members (Bettina Brunner, David Birgmann, Rainer Kasik, Max Nirnberger, Lorenz Prommegger) also teach at various universities in Austria (TU Graz, TU Wien, TU Innsbruck and the Master Class in Architecture at the Art University in Linz). www.xarchitekten.at

## Cover

Photo, front cover © Rupert Asanger
Inside photo, front © Peter Tillessen
Inside photo, back © Iwan Baan

## Photography/image credits

First page © Sandro Hollenstein
Last page © Studio Attersee

Aeby Aumann Emery architectes (p. 84 bottom right)
*Analoge Architektur*, ed. by Miroslav Šik, Boga, Zurich 1987
(p. 16 top right and bottom)
Rupert Asanger (p. 5 top right, p. 76 left)
Iwan Baan (p. 4 top right, pp. 37–43, 99–101)
Adolf Bereuter (p. 107 top centre)
Anna Blau (p. 104 top)
Cortis & Sonderegger (p. 5 bottom left, pp. 56–60)
Eredi Aldo Rossi, Courtesy Fondazione Aldo Rossi
(p. 16 top left)
Martin + Werner Feiersinger (p. 12)
Gina Folly (p. 14)
Roger Frei (pp. 68, 69)
Karin Gauch / Fabien Schwartz (p. 88 top)
Katharina Gossow (p. 109 # 11)
Stéphanie Gygax (p. 3)
Pez Hejduk (p. 104 centre, bottom, p. 105)
Anders Holte (p. 107 bottom left)
Kurt Hörbst (pp. 76, 77)
Hertha Hurnaus (pp. 64, 65)
Doll's house after Arne Jacobsen
(pp. 18 / 19, photography: Thomas Skyum)
Thomas Jantscher (pp. 84, 85)
Miha Krivic (pp. 92, 93)
Michael Lio (p. 107 bottom right)
Iris Meder (p. 106 centre)
Nada Mihajlovic (p. 111 # 25)
Xavier Mora (pp. 31, 32)
Toni Muhr (p. 6)
Taiyo Onorato & Nico Krebs (pp. 20–27)
Österreichische Post (p. 7)
Wladimir Paperny (p. 106 bottom)
Andrew Phelps (pp. 80, 81)
Lorant Racz (p. 110 # 21, p. 111 # 29)
Reiner Riedler (p. 4 left, 28)
Luca Schenardi (p. 10)
Katarina Šoškić (pp. 44–51)
Georg Spitzer (p. 109 # 15)
*Stranger than Paradise* by Jim Jarmusch,
StadtkinoFilmverleih (p. 18 top left)
Joël Tettamanti (p. 19)
Peter Tillessen (p. 5 top left, pp. 52–55)
Udo Titz (p. 106 top)
Claes Westlin (pp. 96, 97)
Wild Club / Session 11 / 11 (pp. 33–35)
Jürg Zimmermann (pp. 9, 72, 73, 88 bottom, pp. 89)

## Concept / Editors / Art Direction

Manuela Hötzl (MaHo), b. 1972, has been writing as an architecture critic and journalist for international architecture and art magazines since 1992 and has edited various book and magazine productions for publishers, firms of architects and other enterprises. She studied architecture in Graz and Pretoria and graduated MA in Research Architecture at the Goldsmiths University of London in 2011. Manuela Hötzl lives and works in Vienna.
www.redaktionsbuero-architektur.at

Kornel Ringli (KoRi), b. 1972, graduated with a diploma in architecture under Prof. Hans Kollhoff at the ETH Zurich in 2001. In addition to working as an architecture critic he also works as communications officer and project developer for the Zurich Immobilienstiftung PWG. At present he is near graduation at the ETH Zurich with a dissertation on Eero Saarinens Terminal for the TWA in New York, supervised by Prof. Dr. Laurent Stalder. Kornel Ringli lives and works in Zurich.

Marco Walser (MaWa), b. 1973, Elektrosmog, studied Visual Commuications at the Zurich University of the Arts, and spent a year in London with an internship at Graphic Thought Facility. Marco Walser teaches at various institutions including the Zurich University of the Arts, the Gerrit Rietveld Academie Amsterdam and the University for Graphics and Arts of the Book in Leipzig. In 1999 he founded the Büro Elektrosmog in Zurich, which he heads as Creative Director. He has received many awards and prizes for book production, including the prize for the Most Beautiful Swiss Books and the Jan Tschichold Prize, 2005. Marco Walser lives and works in Zurich.
www.esmog.org

NiVo • Journal for Architecture
and Cement Composite
Published biannually in German,
English and French
www.nivo-journal.com

Price / single copy
EUR 29.95 (Austria)
EUR 29.13 (Germany)
CHF 36.50 (Switzerland)

Subscriptions and changes
of address
T +41 (0)55 617 11 11
abo@nivo-journal.com

Publisher
FibreCem Holding AG
Eternitstrasse 3
CH-8867 Niederurnen
nivo@fibre-cem.ch
www.fibre-cem.ch
© 2012

Committee
Stefan Cadosch
Philippe Carrard
Christine Dietrich
Anders Holte
Hans-Jörg Kasper
Dietmar Steiner

Editor, Austria
Manuela Hötzl
Gumpendorfer Strasse 46
A-1060 Vienna
maho@nivo-journal.com

Editor, Switzerland
Kornel Ringli
Zurlindenstrasse 277
CH-8003 Zurich
kori@nivo-journal.com

Editorial Assistant
Michael Hasslacher

Correspondent, Germany
Gerwin Zohlen

Correspondents, Slovenia
Maja Vardjan
Jeff Bickert

Art Direction & Design
Elektrosmog, Zurich
Marco Walser, Selina Bütler

Typeface
Fugue (Nivo #1)
by Radim Peško
www.radimpesko.com

Baskerville Original
by Storm Type Foundry
www.stormtype.com

Plan graphics, details
Deck 4 GmbH, Sandra Imfeld

Proofreading
Johannes Payer
(German)

Anna Roos
(English)

Translation
Jean-Pierre Lewerer
(German–French)

Nelson Wattie
(German–English)

David Ender
(English–German)

Copy editing
Véronique Hilfiker Durand
(German)

Jacqueline Dougoud
(English, French)

Printing
DZA Druckerei zu Altenburg, GmbH

© 2012 Springer-Verlag / Vienna
and the contributing writers

Printed in Germany
SpringerWienNewYork is a part of Springer
Science + Business Media
springer.at

SpringerWienNewYork

Product liability: The publisher can give no guar-
antee for the information contained in this book.
The use of registered names, trademarks, etc. in this
publication does not imply, even in the absence of
a specific statement, that such names are exempt
from the relevant protective laws and regulations
and are therefore free for general use.

Printed on acid-free and
chlorine-free bleached paper
Library of Congress Control Number: 2012932407
SPIN: 86073100
With numerous colored images.

ISBN 978-3-7091-1196-3 SpringerWienNewYork

Photo on final page:
Aerial view of Vöcklabruck